P9-DVH-372

# AMERICA AND TWO WARS

By DEXTER PERKINS

HANDS OFF: *A History of the Monroe Doctrine*

AMERICA AND TWO WARS

# AMERICA AND TWO WARS

BY DEXTER PERKINS

LITTLE, BROWN AND COMPANY · BOSTON
1944

FIRST EDITION

*Published June 1944*



PRINTED IN THE UNITED STATES OF AMERICA

# Preface

THE history of American foreign policy during the last thirty years is of vital significance to every American. For the first time in our history as a nation, we have twice in the lives of men of middle age been involved in a world war. To understand how this occurred, to catch the deepest implications of the past and to relate them to the complex and perilous future, this is the duty of every citizen. This little book is a contribution to that end.

I have written the story very briefly and scholars in the field will undoubtedly detect what they deem to be omissions, but it seems to me that what might be most useful today to the individual members of our democracy is not detailed narrative, but some effort at insight into essentials. Long years of study in the field of diplomatic history, I trust I may say also long years of reflection as well, permit me to indulge the hope that these essays, brief as they are, will make clear the large generalizations that have significance for all of us, and by bringing into bold relief the elements of our foreign policy light the way to the wiser handling of the great issues that impend, and that will still be far from solved when the cannon cease to roar, and the bells of all our churches call us once more to rejoice in peace.

In concluding this preface I wish to express my gratitude to Professor Samuel Flagg Bemis, who stands in the forefront of our diplomatic historians, for the careful reading of the manuscript, and to Professor Arthur M. Schlesinger, whose incisive criticism has enriched and improved so many historical enterprises. Both these friends and fellow scholars have been most understanding of what is here attempted; and I hope the book's readers will be no less so.

I must express also my deep appreciation to my secretary, Miss Marjorie Gilles. She has been responsible for most of the mechanics of the work and has taken at all times a lively and personal interest in it, which has been very useful to me.

*March 9, 1944* DEXTER PERKINS

UNIVERSITY OF ROCHESTER

Contents


| | | |
|---|---|---|
| | PREFACE | v |
| I | THE UNITED STATES EMERGES FROM ISOLATION | 3 |
| II | THE FIRST WORLD WAR | 31 |
| III | THE DIPLOMACY OF THE WAR YEARS, 1917–1918 | 53 |
| IV | THE TREATY OF VERSAILLES | 79 |
| V | THE INTERMEDIATE YEARS | 101 |
| VI | THE YEARS OF NONBELLIGERENCY, 1914 AND 1939 | 130 |
| VII | WAR DIPLOMACY, 1941–1943 | 157 |
| VIII | THE PAST, ITS LESSONS, AND THE FUTURE | 183 |
| | INDEX | 207 |

# AMERICA AND TWO WARS

# I

# The United States Emerges from Isolation

*By 1914 the United States had become a world power. It had acquired distant colonies; it had committed itself to long-term policies in the Orient; it was becoming an element in the European balance of power. Its foreign policy was moving away from continentalism and isolationism into a wider sphere.*

## Beginnings

There were many Americans who, down to the seventh of December, 1941, believed that the United States ought to "stay at home and mind its own business." There may be some such still. There may be more of them after the war. Such people have a right to their opinions, of course, but the history of American diplomacy hardly supports them. It demonstrates that for well-nigh half a century the United States has not confined its activities to the American continents, that its people have not wanted to do so, and perhaps that they could not have done so if they wished. This tendency towards a world role may be interrupted, as it has been; it is unlikely that it can be reversed.

It is never possible for the historian to fix an exact date at which a given movement began. History is not so precise as that. But it *is* possible to fix a date that is full of meaning, and that serves as a kind of landmark in a given evolution. The date that marks the emergence of the United States from isolation, its beginnings as a world power, is 1898, the date of the Spanish-American War. Then commenced, generally speaking, the debate between those who wished to confine the role of America within the limits of its surrounding oceans, and those who have insisted, and successfully, as we can see today, upon a broader conception of national policy. It is important for us to remember, however, that the divergence which has been the occasion of so much discussion during the last few decades can hardly be said to have existed at all during most of the nineteenth century.

The purchase of Louisiana in 1803, the purchase of Florida in 1819, the revolt of the American colonies of Spain, reduced, if they did not completely extinguish, the territorial stake of European nations in the New World. There was still Canada, of course; there were Cuba and Puerto Rico; there were the Dutch, the French, the Danish, the British, possessions in the Caribbean. But while American interest in these regions remained, while some of them, particularly Cuba and Canada, became the subject of important diplomatic negotiations and sometimes of genuine solicitude, Americans after 1823 could assume with some degree of assurance that they need not become embroiled in the European politics of the colonial states which still retained a foothold in the New World. Engaged in a vast process of expansion, which carried American population and the American flag from the valley of the Ohio across the Rockies to the Pacific, and created a great republican domain extending from the Great Lakes to the Gulf of Mexico, the people of the United States could well remain preoccupied with their purely continental destiny. While their trade expanded, while their growing economic power became more and more obvious, their foreign commerce was only an unimportant part of their total activity. In circumstances such as these "isolationism" was not a matter of debate; it was the inevitable result of the peculiar circumstances in which the

Americans found themselves, and in which they never ceased to rejoice. The contrary role, that of a world power, to which in due course they would be called, was the violation of a long tradition, the rupture of a deeply rooted habit, the divorcement from a well-understood and much respected past.

The decisive change which was to take place was heralded, as we have said, by the Spanish-American War. Yet there were signs of it before McKinley sent to Congress his special message of April 11, 1898, and these might have been perceived by thoughtful men for some time past. In the seventies for example, two important, in the long run two fateful, events had taken place in the Pacific. American missionaries had been among the first to bring the light of Christianity to the dark-skinned inhabitants of the Hawaiian archipelago, 2000 miles from the American mainland; their descendants, more secular in their ambitions, had built up in the islands a thriving sugar industry. The reciprocity treaty of 1875 gave these producers a favored place in the American market, thus creating an economic bond that was bound in time to have political consequences. Only three years later, the administration of President Hayes signed a treaty with the Samoans, and initiated a tendency which was to carry far, and to demonstrate its full significance only in 1942 and 1943, when the islands of the Samoan group were to furnish the most valuable of steppingstones to the embattled regions of the Far Pacific. Neither the one nor the other of these events was given any very enormous importance at the time, yet both led on to others which have played their part in the development of a more ambitious American policy. By 1887 the Americans of Hawaii had secured, by the constitution adopted in that year, a substantial measure of control over the politics of this independent kingdom; and when in 1893 the last of the Hawaiian monarchs, the ill-fated Liliuokalani, made a feeble and abortive attempt to regain some of the power which her Kanaka compatriots had surrendered, the result was a revolution which drove her from power, established a republican government in control of some of the most influential white men in the islands, and was followed by a treaty of annexation signed by the new republic with the government of the United States. The treaty, it is true, came in the last days of the Harrison administration; Grover Cleveland, Mr. Harrison's successor, upholder of the conservative traditions in foreign affairs, troubled, too, by the feeling that the American Minister in Hawaii had been the accomplice of the revolutionists, withdrew the treaty from the Senate; and, with the resolute conviction that was characteristic of him, refused to press the matter in any way whatever. But a new issue had been made up, nonetheless, and it was difficult to imagine that even the granite will of a great President could indefinitely postpone a favorable decision on the question of annexation. In much the same fashion events had drawn the United States into a novel situation in Samoa. The existence of American interests there, along with those of Germany and Great Britain, had been productive of no little friction; and in 1889 an arrangement had been made which called for joint control of the islands by the three rival powers. Mr. Cleveland, when he came into office, harshly criticized this arrangement as a violation of American tradition; but he did not go so far as to upset it, and its continued existence provided new evidence that the diplomatic interests of the United States were widening with time.

These widening interests, it can now be demonstrated, were after all the reflection of a change of national mood. Nations, like individuals, have their periods of depression or inertia, or of satisfaction with things as they are; like individuals, also, they have their periods of buoyancy, of energy, of eager searching for a larger role in the world. It needs very little knowledge of the political literature of the late eighties and early nineties to perceive that a new and more ambitious epoch for the United States was on its way. One of the most popular of contemporary American historians, John Fiske, one of the most distinguished of American political scientists, John W. Burgess, one of the most widely read of American clergymen, Josiah Strong, the most influential of American naval commentators, Alfred Thayer Mahan, all combined, in the period we are mentioning, to do homage to the genius of their country, and to predict for it a new and wider destiny. Nor were they without support from the politicians of the time. There was more than a touch of the grandiose in the foreign policy of James G. Blaine, a veteran Republican, and twice Secretary of State of the United States; but Blaine's calculated aggressiveness paled into insignificance in comparison with the ardor of two younger men, both destined to play a great part in the affairs of their party and of the nation. Henry Cabot Lodge, the scholar in politics, as Massachusetts loved to call him, was from the very period of his entry into the Senate the advocate of a strong foreign policy; and his young friend Theodore Roosevelt, so suggestively described by Henry Adams as "pure act," was eager, as the Venezuela crisis of 1895 demonstrated, to find opportunity for the expression of his monumental energy upon the field of battle. Even more important and significant, the mood of the country communicated itself to President Cleveland, stolid, unimaginative, and conservative, as that great figure was known to be. In his second administration an insignificant boundary dispute between Great Britain and Venezuela was magnified into a major political issue; arbitration of the difference was demanded by the United States; and when Lord Salisbury, with a complacency altogether characteristic, long neglected to reply to the American demands, and, replying late, challenged the viewpoint of the administration, the President sent a special message to Congress in which he declared that if the British government did not agree to the arbitral settlement of the dispute, he would appoint a commission to determine the proper boundary, and would, if necessary, carry out its findings with all the power of the United States. The Cleveland message, though denounced by many "intellectuals" and churchmen, was received with widespread applause in the great body of American opinion; and though the question with which it dealt was finally settled by compromise, and a substantial retreat on the part of Great Britain, the whole episode expressed a national mood for which it would be difficult to find a parallel at any time in the twenty years preceding.

Nor was this the only question that troubled the tranquillity of the American people; in 1895 insurrection broke out in Cuba, at our very doors, and as the struggle there widened, and became marked by great ferocity, there arose a clamor for some action in favor of the insurgents. On this point Mr. Cleveland, it is true, was adamant; and he was able to pursue a dignified and restrained policy until the very end of his administration. But the Republicans, in their party platform of 1896, paid due homage to the rising impatience of the American people and to the change in national temper; and they called, in ringing language, not only for the independence of Cuba, but for the assertion of the Monroe Doctrine, the annexation of Hawaii, the purchase of the Danish West Indies, the construction of an interoceanic canal, and even for affirmative action to stop the massacres which were then going on in Armenia, in a region which had not generally been regarded as of particular interest to the people of the United States. True, they chose as their candidate for the

Presidency a man whose whole personality was saturated with amiability, and who hardly seemed the prototype of a war President; but William McKinley, whatever his personal predilections, was hardly the type of man who could be expected to stay the march of a popular movement, or successfully to "ride the whirlwind and direct the storm."

## The Spanish-American War

We need not enter into detail with regard to the events that led to the war with Spain; the sympathy of the American people with the Cuban insurgents grew with time; the sinking of the American battleship *Maine* in Havana Harbor, whatever may have lain behind it, provided a popular catchword for the advocates of war; the Spanish government yielded too little and too late to American importunities for a settlement of the Cuban question; the Cubans themselves in any case would probably have continued the struggle until they forced American intervention on the basis of independence; and the administration, in April of 1898, found itself compelled to take action and embark on a war in which it was to be brilliantly successful, and which it was to win at a very small cost indeed in treasure or in lives.

As with many another struggle, the consequences of the war of 1898 could hardly have been foreseen; and it would have been difficult to predict that the first great news the American people had of the action of their armed forces would come not from the waters of the Caribbean, but from the other side of the Pacific. There were not many Americans who knew or cared about the Philippines in 1898; but they were soon to be made aware of them through the action of the Assistant Secretary of the Navy, Theodore Roosevelt. The order of February 25, 1898, by which this energetic young administrator, during the absence of his superior from office, directed the squadron of Admiral Dewey, then at Hong Kong, to take offensive action against the islands in the event of war has been often commented upon; it was followed out as soon as practicable; and the battle of Manila provided the Americans of that generation with the greatest thrill which they had had in many a long day. The event was destined, however, to be more than thrilling; as time went on, it proved to be nothing short of momentous; and when the peace protocol with Spain was signed in August of 1898, the most perplexing and the most far-reaching problem involved in the ending of the war was the disposition to be made of Spain's colonial possession on the other side of the Pacific. It was a foregone conclusion, on the whole, that Cuba should be given the freedom which the United States had pledged her; it was elementary to take possession of the island of Puerto Rico, so conveniently located in the Caribbean; but it was not so easy to decide what to do with territories thousands of miles away even from our own Pacific coast, and the very existence or location of which had been most imperfectly known to most Americans before the outbreak of war. In deciding this great question, President McKinley had recourse both to prayer and to public opinion; and fortunately for his own peace of mind he was similarly instructed by Providence and by what he thought to be the feeling of the people of the United States. It was decided to demand the surrender of the islands by Spain; the disconsolate emissaries of the government at Madrid were cheered by the payment of $20,000,000 for the cession; and with the completion of the compact there opened one of the greatest political debates in the history of the United States.

For here, indeed, was a breach with the past that was full of large implications; here, indeed, was the decisive moment when the United States forsook for all time the role of a continental power and entered upon a course of action that was, in due time, to cause Americans to die in the fastnesses of Bataan, and to resist to the last in the rock galleries of Corregidor.

The fight against the ratification of the peace treaty, as twenty years later in the case of the treaty of Versailles, was to be in some degree disfigured by partisanship; but no such charge can be brought against such a devoted Republican as Senator George Frisbie Hoar of Massachusetts, who contended with vigor against the course of the administration. To Senator Hoar, the acquisition of the Philippines was a breach with the past too grave to be palliated; it involved the abandonment, in his view, of basic American conceptions of freedom and self-government; by involving the United States in affairs far beyond its borders, it jeopardized the traditional foreign policy of the United States, and invited Europe to interfere in the affairs of the New World. There were other Senators, some of them Democrats, who held this view with equal sincerity and intensity; and in one sense of the term, the debate of the end of '98 and the early days of '99 was the opening engagement in the long strife between "isolationists" and "interventionists," to use the cant phrases of today, which has had such profound effects upon the development of American foreign policy. For though the issue, it is true, was not European, and might at first blush seem to have little to do with our entanglement in European affairs, what was really involved was an attitude of mind, a choice between enlarged and restricted responsibility; and while it is by no means true that those who favored the annexation of the Philippines in 1898 were necessarily or inevitably to be the advocates of a militant policy toward Germany in the years 1914–1918, or convinced believers in international co-operation in 1919 and 1920, it is nonetheless the fact that in the long run a policy of expansion in the Orient, and that of increased participation in European affairs, must stand or fall together. Of this, Americans of 1944 ought to be painfully aware, as they witness the association of Japanese and German militarism, and contend at one and the same time against the disturbers of peace in the Pacific and the disturbers of the peace in Europe.

The victory in the struggle over the peace treaty, though difficult (Henry Cabot Lodge declared it to be the "closest and hardest fight" in which he had been engaged), was to go to the administration. The leader of the Democratic Party, William Jennings Bryan, from either partisan calculation, true patriotism, or a mixture of the one and the other, induced some of his followers in the Senate to vote for ratification; it may be, too, that the outbreak of insurrection in the Philippines just before the decision was taken contributed to the result; at any rate, the treaty was finally approved by the very close vote of fifty-seven to twenty-seven. A change of only two votes, it will be observed, would have delayed, though it might not have prevented, the triumph of the administration; while a resolution expressly promising independence to the inhabitants of the Philippines was defeated only by the casting vote of the Vice-President, a fact which demonstrated that many Americans were reluctant to embark upon that "large policy" or recognize that sense of a wider destiny which, as we have seen, had played so great a part in the thinking of Henry Cabot Lodge, and, still more important, in that of Theodore Roosevelt, soon to be President of the United States.

Nonetheless the decision had been taken; and it was one of immense importance. *By the ratification of the treaty of peace with Spain, the United States became a Pacific power; it could no longer remain indifferent to what went on there; it had taken up responsibilities, not only for the development of the Filipinos, but for their protection from aggression. The pledge has had to be redeemed in our own day.*

## The Open Door Policy

The same administration which made peace with Spain laid down principles of action with regard to China that were to have far-reaching effects. One of the arguments used in connection with the taking of the Philippines was that the possession of those islands would open the way to the commercial conquest of the Orient; and in the very years during which we were debating the Filipino question the future of the great Chinese Empire was a matter of solicitude and discussion. It seemed as if that Empire might be partitioned; the powers of Europe were busily seeking special privileges within its borders; and influenced by these facts the American Secretary of State, John Hay, came forward with his famous doctrine of the Open Door, which was aimed at preserving equality of opportunity in the great markets of the East. It is not true, as has sometimes been stated, and as Americans in their romantic moods like to believe, that the Hay notes prevented the breakup of China; but it *is* true that they set forth doctrines to which the United States has since usually adhered. These seemed to be doctrines of peace; but they inevitably raised the question of what the United States would do if they were challenged. That question, like the colonial question, had much to do with what was to happen in the years from 1937 to 1941.

Nor was this all. When an anti-foreign revolt broke out in China, and the representatives of the great powers were besieged at Peking, American troops joined with those of Europe in marching to the relief of the legations. The American government played a part in the negotiations that followed the military operations, and while it is clear that it was troubled by the fear of criticism at home, it is also clear that it was by no means disposed to be silent so far as Far Eastern questions were concerned.

*There was no time, indeed, after 1898 when the United States was not vitally interested in the question of China. Few people realized what that interest might eventually imply, that it might mean that some day the Americans would be called to fight for the principles they proposed to maintain; but fewer still condemned those principles, or were ready to express the opinion that they ought never to have been put forward.*

## Naval Expansion

In the years from 1898 to 1914 American foreign policy was neither, as of old, entirely confined to the American continents in its diplomatic action, nor was it yet based upon a complete consciousness of America's possible role as a world power. One striking change, already under way, was much accentuated by the Spanish War. Secure on their continental island, threatened from no quarter, the beneficiaries of a peace which owed much to the domination of Great Britain upon the seas in the nineteenth and early twentieth centuries, and for which they did not have to pay, the people of the United States had found it hard to realize that force had played and might again play a large part in international affairs. The illusion that peace might rest upon benevolent moral sentiments, the Victorian superstition (how else shall we qualify it today?) that the world was growing better so rapidly that it would soon have no need of war, was nowhere more ardently believed than in this country. In the nineties this attitude had begun to change; and not only were notable steps taken towards building up the navy in the Harrison and the second Cleveland administration, but the policy of naval construction was altered much for the better. No more profound error can be committed in military or naval policy than the error of basing one's action upon a purely defensive conception of war. We have had the most striking illustration of this within the last three years in the collapse of France; but the Maginot Line psychology, if I may call it that, is a very old one — and almost uniformly disastrous. For many decades it conditioned American naval construction, leading to the ridiculous gunboat policy of the Jeffersonian period, and to an emphasis upon commerce-destroying vessels at a later date. But in the 1890's largely under the spur of Mahan, the spirit began to change, and the way was cleared for the construction of battleships powerful enough to go to meet the enemy, and to carry on operations at some distance from the American coast. The United States entered the war with Spain with a navy built and building much larger than at any time since the Civil War; and its exploits were a matter of much popular pride. In such an atmosphere, it was possible to push still further a program of naval expansion; the advent of Roosevelt to the Presidency meant that for the first time the Chief Executive of the Nation was eagerly, ardently and intelligently interested in an efficient and adequate force upon the seas; the formation of the Navy League in 1903 was a sign of popular interest, even though cynics suggested that some of its supporters were acting from ulterior motives; and by 1914 American naval power, though far behind that of Great Britain and substantially behind that of Germany, was greater than it had been at any period in the history of the Republic. The conservatives of the epoch, farmers of the Middle West and the South, pacifists in New England, declared that all this building was ridiculous, that nobody threatened or could threaten the security of the United States, and if the allusion was to direct physical conquest, their argument was cogent; but to such logic two answers could readily be given. In the larger question of foreign policy the weight that the United States would carry would surely stand in some relation to the physical force which it already possessed and was ready to exert; and, in addition to this, it was not to be forgotten that the defense not only of the Philippines, but of Hawaii (annexed in July, 1898) and the Samoan Islands (part of which were definitely acquired in 1899), imposed upon this country new and inescapable responsibilities. On the whole, then, the advocates of a larger navy, though frequently hard-pressed, and sometimes defeated, got at least a part of their way in the years after the Spanish War, and the recognition of the fact that force, whether one likes it or not, does play an important part in international relations had, in some measure, been more fully recognized by a large part of the American people.

## The United States and the Politics of Europe

The year 1898 is not only the year of decisive events for the United States in the area of the Pacific; it is also the year from which we may conveniently date the European developments which culminated in the war of 1914. It was in 1898 that Imperial Germany, already the most prosperous and vigorous power on the continent of Europe, began the construction of a great navy; and it was Germany's decision on this point which did much to awaken Great Britain from that complacent insularity into which she had fallen under Lord Salisbury, and which she was later to fall into under Mr. Stanley Baldwin. The result, in due time, and by the slow and often tortuous processes of diplomacy, was the so-called Cordial Understanding between France and Great Britain in 1904; and the effort of Germany to test, or to sound out, this understanding produced the Moroccan crisis of 1905. In that year war was, indeed, averted, but the realignment of European states was carried further; and in 1907 France was able to reconcile her older partner and ally, Czarist Russia, with her new-won friend across the Channel. The Cordial Understanding of 1904 thus became the Triple Entente of 1907; and Germany and her ally Austria-Hungary found themselves confronted with a developing coalition. It is true that, in theory, they did not stand alone; the Kingdom of Italy was, the language of treaties affirmed, a member of the so-called Triple Alliance; but the value of Italian friendship was not to be too confidently counted upon. The malaise in the chancelleries of Berlin and Vienna increased as time went on; and beginning in 1908 a series of diplomatic crises gave warning of an approaching storm. In the year just named Austria annexed Bosnia and Herzegovina (provinces entrusted to her administration by the treaty of Berlin), to the great discontent of the Russians and Serbs. In 1911 Germany again tested out the situation in Morocco, and conflict was only narrowly averted; in 1912 and 1913 the Balkan Wars troubled the relations of the larger European states, and set the nerves of the diplomats on edge. In this atmosphere of increasing tension, as we now view it in retrospect, and with secure knowledge, it was probable that some reckless act would sooner or later provoke an explosion; and the reckless act came when a Bosnian patriot, Gabrio Princip, on the twenty-eighth of June, 1914, took the life of the heir to the Austrian throne, the Archduke Francis Ferdinand, at Sarajevo. What followed we all know: the Austrian ultimatum to Serbia, which state was held responsible (not without reason) for the assassination, since the plot against the Archduke took place on her soil; the invasion of this little country by the troops of the Dual Monarchy; the mobilization of Russia; the German ultimatum to the Czar; the declaration of war by the Reich on August 1; the inevitable inclusion of France, Russia's ally, in the struggle; the German violation of Belgian neutrality; the entry of Great Britain into the war.

Such, in brief, is the story of the coming of the First World War. In these years of mounting danger, what was the position of the United States? Speaking broadly, it cannot be said that the American people at all understood what was happening in Europe. There existed in this country a romantic notion that war, at any rate war on a large scale, was a thing of the past, inconsistent with an advanced civilization and an increasing economic interdependence; many Americans had read Norman Angell's *Great Illusion,* which demonstrated the folly, nay, the impossibility of what was about to happen; the succession of European crises seemed to cheerful people to indicate that no nation would take the final step, rather than that the final step was drawing near. In general, the attitude of the mass of Americans was reflected by the government in power, but there was one exception to this general rule. Theodore Roosevelt, it must be conceded, saw further than many others; he seems to have had some conception of what a general European war might mean to the United States; and he played, therefore, an active role in the European crisis of 1905. On the thirty-first of March of that year the German Emperor, on a cruise in the Mediterranean, landed at Tangier and made a speech stressing his interest in the independence of Morocco. His pronouncement was a direct challenge to the ambition of France to a protectorate over that country, and produced a serious diplomatic situation. Great Britain rallied to the side of her diplomatic partner; the outlook was ominous. In such a dangerous situation President Roosevelt did his best to bring about a peaceful solution of the problem; he was wise enough and farsighted enough to see that the United States had a direct interest in the avoidance of a general European war. That his activities were decisive is not likely; France had its appeasers in 1905, as in 1938; and the resignation of the French Foreign Minister, M. Delcassé, paved the way for the calling of an international conference at Algeciras. But, significantly and without precedent, the American government was represented at this conference, and its influence was exerted in favor of France. While the solution of the Moroccan question was not in conformity with the American proposals, the participation of our diplomats in the settlement was the symbol of an attitude very different from the traditional one. It represented the beginning of a wider policy in regard to European affairs.

But the action of Roosevelt stands alone. When the Act of Algeciras came before the Senate of the United States for ratification, a reservation was attached declaring that there was no purpose "to depart from the traditional American foreign policy which forbids participation by the United States in the settlement of political questions which are entirely European in their scope." This action was no doubt fairly typical of American public opinion; and in the years from 1908 to 1914 it was reflected in the policy of the United States in general. In 1910, for example, when the stormy petrel of the American Navy, Admiral Sims, declared in a speech at the Mansion House in London that the British in an emergency could always count on their "kindred" across the sea, he was sharply reprimanded by President Taft himself; and the crisis of 1911, the Italian-Tripolitan War, the Balkan Wars that succeeded, drew from the President no other public comment than that these were matters "without direct political concern" or "interest" to the United States. The Presidential campaign of 1912 turned almost exclusively upon questions of domestic policy; the Democratic President who entered the White House in 1913 was bent not upon an ambitious foreign policy, but upon internal reform. True, he did send his confidant and friend, Colonel E. M. House, to Europe to try by secret negotiations to draw Great Britain and Germany together, and these negotiations were actually proceeding almost at the moment of the outbreak of war; there was a certain boldness and largeness of view in such a plan, but that the Colonel had any clear idea of the immense difficulty of the problem or of the vast forces involved does not appear from his *Intimate Papers.* In his public addresses, President Wilson gave no intimation of the perils ahead; nor did William Jennings Bryan, his Secretary of State. The tone of both these men, when war came, was one of surprise and horror. In this they were no different from the mass of the American people.

*But despite American ignorance of the gravity of the hour, and despite American disinclination to take part in the politics of Europe, the period 1898–1914 did much to shape the course of action when war came. Americans did not know it, but they were becoming a part of the world balance of power; their favor was being courted by both Great Britain and Germany; and they themselves were making up their minds as to their preference between these two powers. Let us examine this situation in a little more detail and look more closely at our relations with the first of the powers just mentioned, Great Britain.*

## Anglo-American Relations, 1898–1914

Among the popular legends that hamper an understanding of the foreign policy of the United States is the legend that the Americans are an innocent and naïve people, who are constantly being duped by others more subtle and less scrupulous. This legend, in a more specialized form, maintains that American diplomacy has constantly been the victim of the wiles of Great Britain. In this form it is, of course, particularly acceptable to those elements of our population who, for one reason or another, have never loved our British cousins. It is, however, very far indeed from the truth; and no one who studies the facts with candor can reasonably maintain that we were led either into the First or into the Second World War by the wicked wiles of the Court of St. James's. Yet it is true that the British were the first to recognize the full bearings of the Spanish-American War on the role of the United States as a world power; and it is true also that in the years from 1898 to 1914 British diplomacy built up a great reserve of good will in the United States that was undoubtedly to be of value when the struggle finally broke out.

Before 1898 British and American relations cannot be said to have been precisely cordial for any long period at a time. While the two countries had fought but once since the war of the American Revolution, there was scarcely a decade when they had not had a sharp difference of opinion, if not a heated controversy; and tradition, and the prejudices of very large elements of our immigrant population, operated for a long time to keep alive some feeling of distrust, if not of hostility. In 1895, as we have already seen, in the administration of Grover Cleveland, a particularly acrimonious exchange of views took place; but interestingly enough, the very intensity of the difference paved the way for the beginnings of an understanding which had progressed far indeed by the outbreak of the First World War. The President and his combative Secretary of State, Richard Olney, were themselves influenced by the abrupt change in the public mood which followed on the events of December, 1895; and coincident with the settlement of the Venezuela boundary controversy went the negotiation of a treaty of arbitration framed on broader lines than any to which any American diplomat had yet affixed his signature. True, the resulting compact did not reach the Senate till McKinley came into office; and before that august body it suffered the fate which was more and more to be reserved for understandings of this kind. But the gesture was a useful one; and the victory of the Republican Party and the gold standard in the elections of 1896 could not fail to be gratifying to influential circles in London, the money market of the world, and the source of much of the capital which had been used in the development of the United States. The British, then, were in a reasonably good mood with regard to this country when the war with Spain began; and during the struggle they alone of all the great European countries were quick to express their sympathetic understanding of the position taken by the American government. In Continental Europe the general feeling with regard to the war was one of cynicism, mixed with dynastic fellow feeling for the Spanish monarchy, and, on the part of France, solicitude for investments in the Spanish peninsula; but in Great Britain the attitude was entirely different, and all the more appreciated because it was not observable elsewhere. There were even voices in London which dared pronounce the word "alliance," and among these was the voice of Joseph Chamberlain, Colonial Secretary in the ministry of Lord Salisbury. For Britain the period of splendid isolation was coming to an end; the search for friends and close associates in the international arena was definitely beginning; and between 1898 and 1914 British diplomacy went out of its way to win the good graces of the United States. There was, in this, nothing that can faintly be described as sinister; it was wise, it was honest, it was provident; it is to be deprecated only by those who definitely repudiate the proposition that the friendly association of the two great Anglo-Saxon peoples may be of immense service not only to themselves, but to world stability and world progress as well.

The steps in the courtship, if the term be not too extreme, deserve to be recorded; and perhaps the first of them was the consent given by Great Britain to the abrogation of the Clayton-Bulwer Treaty of April 19, 1850, which provided for a joint control of an interoceanic canal. Ever since the Civil War this treaty had proved irksome to American opinion; the feeling had been sharpened as the idea of a canal began to enter the sphere of practical reality with the inauguration of De Lesseps' famous enterprise at Panama in 1879, and a prolonged diplomatic controversy over the compact of 1850 had taken place in the early eighties. The war with Spain and the acquisition of the Philippines only pointed the lesson of the necessity of a canal, a canal under American control; and, seeing that this mattered immensely to the Americans, the British wisely agreed, without asking anything in return, to a new treaty, the so-called Hay-Pauncefote Treaty, by which the United States was given a large part of what it was seeking. When, moreover, the resulting accord was amended by the Senate of the United States, largely because it did not concede to the United States the right to fortify the projected international waterway, the British, after some initial annoyance, consented to a new and improved compact, even more favorable to American aspirations. Such complacency, or generosity (call it what you will), is unusual in diplomacy, and not particularly conspicuous in the diplomacy of Great Britain.

In 1902 the British and German governments undertook a punitive blockade of the coast of Venezuela, then ruled by one of the most odious of Latin-American dictators; though American consent had been secured beforehand, the incident stirred up a good deal of feeling in the United States; and as this became increasingly patent, the British press and public men made haste to adjust their tone to American prejudice. Almost with one accord they proclaimed their admiration for and support of the Monroe Doctrine; and the respect which they paid to this fundamental American principle could not fail to promote the growth of friendly feeling between the two nations.

At much the same time there existed a dispute between the American and Canadian governments with regard to the Alaskan boundary; the influence of London was exerted to see to it that the dispute was referred to arbitration; and in the ensuing proceedings once again the Court of St. James's strove to gratify the authorities at Washington. The American representation on the six-man body which dealt with the dispute can hardly be said to have been remarkable for its judicial detachment; and perhaps two of the three representatives on the other side, both Canadians, were no less partial. But the sixth member of the tribunal was Lord Alverstone, the Lord Chief Justice of England, who not only cast the deciding vote in favor of the American contentions, but was also, as we now know, in close contact with the Foreign Office, and in part guided by their views. That Great Britain should risk the discontent of one of the most important of her Dominions to satisfy American feeling was striking evidence of the depth of her desire for a good understanding with the government at Washington.

In the Orient, it is true, the British were not quite so ready to march with the United States. British influence accounted, in part, for the Open Door notes of Secretary Hay; but the enthusiasm of Downing Street for the American policy was never very marked, and by 1902 it had become clear, on the other hand, that London could not count upon the active and continuous support of the United States for the protection of its own interests in the Far East. The Anglo-Japanese alliance was the result; and in the following years, and indeed down almost to the outbreak of the Second World War, the Foreign Office was, on more than one occasion, divided between a desire to maintain its connection with Japan and the desire to win the good will of the United States. A partial answer to its difficulties, however, was discovered when the Anglo-Japanese alliance was renewed for the second time in 1911; on that occasion a special clause was inserted by which neither of the contracting parties was obliged to go to war with any nation with which it had a general treaty of arbitration. The British hastened to negotiate such a treaty with the United States; and although the Senate amended the resulting document so viciously as to destroy it, the gesture of friendship still remained. Moreover, when the Wilson administration came into power, a new formula presented itself. Mr. Bryan, the Secretary of State, attached great importance to what he described as cooling-off treaties by which the contracting parties agreed to submit all disputes to investigation or arbitration before resort to war; the British agreed readily to the negotiation of such a treaty; and they even went so far as to declare to the Japanese government and to that of the United States that such a treaty was a treaty of arbitration within the meaning of the Anglo-Japanese alliance of 1911.

In the opening years of the Wilson administration, it is true, two rather vexing questions for a little disturbed the cordial relations of the two governments; on the one hand, Great Britain regarded legislation exempting American coastal shipping from tolls in the Panama Canal as contrary to the Hay-Pauncefote Treaty of 1901, and requested its repeal; on the other hand, the Wilson administration was irked at Great Britain's recognition of the Mexican government of General Huerta, which had come into power by a bloody *coup d'état,* and which, on this ground, Woodrow Wilson and William Jennings Bryan firmly declined to recognize; but the friction that resulted was of short duration. With high courage, and a stern sense of obligation to the pledged word, President Wilson demanded and obtained from Congress the repeal of the

obnoxious statute on canal tolls; the British ceased to interest themselves in the Mexican dictator, and the diplomatic skies were again serene. In 1914 the peace societies in both countries were preparing to celebrate a century of peace between the two kindred nations; the American-Canadian frontier, it was proudly pointed out, was the longest undefended frontier in the world; the common heritage of the two countries in law, in literature, in learning, was the favorite theme of many an after-dinner speech on both sides of the water; and the impending passage of the Irish Home Rule Bill by the British Parliament seemed likely to eliminate, or at any rate to reduce, one of the most serious remaining sources of division between the two peoples. Taking things all in all, the relations of the two countries had rarely been better; and looking back over the years 1898 to 1914, there had been no period of equal length in which they had been so good. That this was a fact of importance when it came to the outbreak of the World War no thoughtful man is likely to gainsay.

## German-American Relations, 1898–1914

In the same period there had grown up a very different and somewhat unfriendly feeling with regard to Germany. The strength of this must not be exaggerated, but its actual existence can hardly be denied. Memories partly well-founded, partly imagined, prejudices dimly felt but never absent, clashes of interest far from fundamental but by no means unreal, contributed to diminish cordiality if not to create actual tension in the relations of the United States and the German Reich. Americans remembered, for example, that in the summer of 1898 the Germans had sent to Manila Bay a naval squadron rivaling that of Admiral Dewey in size; and many of them believed that a clash between this force, under the command of Admiral Diederichs, and the victor of Manila had narrowly been averted. They observed, too, that at the end of the Spanish-American War the Caroline Islands had come into the hands of Germany, and could not help suspecting (rightly enough) that the Germans had had their eyes also upon the Philippines. Their interpretation of these facts may have been somewhat garbled; indeed careful investigation suggests that German policy was, in most respects, formally correct; but the rumors that circulated in the United States were more influential than history itself, and if they owed something to invention, and possibly something to British jealousy, the fact ought not to be regarded as curious. Nor did the question of the Philippines stand alone. At the turn of the century, there existed the belief (now rendered doubtful by historical research) that sinister German influences lay behind the failure of the Danish Rigsdag to ratify the treaty for the cession of the Danish West Indies (the present Virgin Islands); more important still, American public opinion was deeply disturbed by the Venezuelan blockade of 1902. It is true that both the British and the Germans took part in this easily comprehensible enterprise; it is even true that the fleets of both nations resorted to bombardment of the Venezuelan coast; but the indignation of the American people fell with peculiar weight upon Germany. For the British, quickly sensing the situation, as we have already seen, proceeded by soft words to turn away wrath; and while their statesmen were ostentatiously recognizing the Monroe Doctrine, the German press was engaged in a philippic against the United States, and the German Foreign Office was unable to match British complacency with a no less unreserved acceptance of the cardinal principle of American foreign policy. It intended nothing ill; it was well aware of the problem; but it dared not make the wise and necessary gesture, and out of the events of 1902 there grew the legend, already in process of development by

1907, that President Roosevelt had delivered an ultimatum to the government of Berlin, and forced it at the point of the sword, one might say, to desist from a wicked enterprise of conquest. This utterly inaccurate reminiscence owed much to the temper of the President himself; but the high authority of his name gave the appearance of veracity to what must, alas! be regarded as one of the least attractive examples of his extraordinary egotism, and of his vivid and sometimes uncontrolled imagination.

In addition to all these stories there were other reasons why the relations of the United States with the Reich should not be of unmixed happiness. German naval circles were becoming more aggressive with time; they undoubtedly had their eyes on various choice sites in the Caribbean, and elsewhere on this side of the Atlantic; and American naval officers were keenly aware of this and undoubtedly tended to think in competitive terms of the navy that was rising across the seas. German Pan-German literature dwelt much upon the numbers and influence of the large German population of Brazil; and while this was not in any sense official, it could not fail to be disquieting. German trade relations with the United States were highly competitive; Americans, though protectionist themselves, resented the high tariffs levied against them in the interests of the *Junkers;* and in other markets they found the Germans troublesome, aggressive and ingenious rivals.

As time went on, moreover, it was not difficult to represent the German Empire as a militarist power, whose ideals were out of accord with those of the United States. The people of this country have always believed themselves to be pacific; they were never more firmly convinced of the fact than in the decade after the war with Spain. The severity of the Germans in the Far East, at the time of the Boxer revolt, shocked

Americans, as did the allusions of the German Emperor to the yellow peril; when the Germans took, as they did, a somewhat obstructive attitude at the second Hague Conference with regard to the problems of disarmament, the fact was duly noted in the United States; so, too, was the unwillingness of Germany to sign one of Mr. Taft's arbitration treaties, or one of the cooling-off treaties of Mr. Bryan; while the Zabern affair of 1913, in which Prussian soldiery were accused of the brutal treatment of an Alsatian shoemaker, produced much criticism from the American press. The mystical language of the Kaiser, with its curious harking back to the divine right of sovereigns, could hardly fail to provoke ridicule, if not resentment here; and while no one of these things was of first importance, it does not seem unreasonable to imagine that they produced their effects, and contributed to the bias of American opinion.

This is by no means to say that German foreign policy in these years was definitely hostile to the United States. The German Foreign Office, as a matter of fact, was keenly aware of the desirability of American friendship; it naturally feared close American relations with Great Britain, and the Kaiser himself, especially in the Rooseveltian era, exhausted himself in blandishments with regard to the occupant of the White House and the people whose destinies he guided. In 1902 he sent his brother, Prince Henry, on a special mission of friendship to this country; he was helpful to a degree in bringing about the successful diplomatic intervention of the President in the Russo-Japanese War, an intervention which brought about peace and won for its author the Nobel Peace Prize; he attempted to arrive at a concert of action with the American government in the affairs of the Orient; he took the advice of Washington, or at any rate appeared to do so, in connection with the Moroccan crisis of 1905. Made aware by the Venezuelan blockade of the sensitiveness of American opinion to any use of force in the New World, the German Foreign Office behaved with great caution in the years following 1903; it sent a close friend of the President to represent German interests at Washington, and for more than a decade it avoided any direct challenge to American feelings. But all these efforts seemed, for some reason or other, to fall short of their goal; they were outweighed by the considerations already discussed; and there is no doubt that they left the German government in a relatively disadvantageous position as compared with Great Britain. At the outbreak of the First World War there already existed in the United States, though not of course in all quarters or amongst all elements of the population, not only a widespread predilection for Great Britain but a distrust of her rapidly growing rival.

## Summary

*In 1914, then, the American people had taken the first steps along the road that they are following today. They had enlarged their interests, and had become a Great Power in a new sense of the term; they had a territorial stake in the Far Pacific; they had their ideas as to the future destiny of China, and some desire to play a part in that destiny; they were enlarging their navy; they had, on at least one occasion, taken part in a European political conference; and they did not view all European powers with the same degree of warmth. Whether they knew it or not, they were in a mood to take sides if war came.*

*This brief analysis of the years 1898–1914 illustrates a stream of tendency. The "isolationist" of recent years may have had an argument for his viewpoint, but the most accurate thing to say about him is that he was outdated. Events of the past, a past that extended as far back as 1898, had already prepared for America another course and another future.*

# II

# The First World War

## American Neutrality

*From the outbreak of the World War in 1914, American majority opinion desired the victory of the Allies. For this reason, and because it was a striking violation of existing international law and standards of humanity, the submarine warfare was harshly judged—and opposed. This issue brought the United States into the war. The decision for war was a national decision, not the personal decision of Woodrow Wilson. The story of these years demonstrates the difficulty of remaining aloof from a great international conflict.*

## Why We Entered the War

*The war which began in Europe in August, 1914, was, in the course of less than three years, to involve the United States and usher in an unprecedented chapter in American history. In February of 1915, the German Imperial Government began its submarine campaign against Great Britain. The American government contested the legality of this warfare from the outset, and maintained that its rights as a neutral had been violated. Despite a succession of incidents, of which the most dramatic and decisive was the sinking of the* Lusitania, *with the loss of 128 American lives, President Wilson was able, in the spring of 1916, to bring about a temporary cessation of such acts. But in February, 1917, the authorities at Berlin re-*

*newed the underseas warfare, in unrestricted form. There followed an immediate severance of relations, and after two months of suspense the entry of the United States into the war. Such, reduced to the very simplest terms, is the story of the events leading up to our participation in the momentous struggle of a quarter of a century ago.*

At a later date, certain historians and publicists had much to add to this simple explanation. The decision to go to war, they maintained, was due to a variety of other reasons—to a wicked and calculating British propaganda, to the swollen profits of those engaged in the munitions trade, to the vast loans that were made to the governments of the Allies. Convinced, as some of these men were, that our entry into the war was a gigantic mistake, they looked around and found what they were looking for, a theory to fit their needs, and to make American action appear stupid, or mercenary. And their view, much to our own misfortune, was accepted by many persons, especially by many who did not remember the events of 1914–1917, and who therefore, in a period of reaction, could easily be convinced of the folly or the greed of those who preceded them.

The flaws in the arguments of the "revisionists," if so they might be called, were many and flagrant. For example, it is clear that the unrestricted submarine campaign was the *occasion* of the United States entering the war against Germany. But if this is so, how can it possibly be proved that the decision for war would ever have been taken *without* that campaign? How can anyone *know* that, had Germany minded her manners, we would have gone to war over trade, or to save the war debts, or under the impulse of an educational campaign launched overseas? There can be no satisfactory answer to this question.

But let us look a little further into this matter. Let us take, for example, the argument that Americans were propagandized into war. This argument is based upon the assumption that there really was not much difference between one side and the other, at the outset, and that the people of the United States were misled into taking sides by calculating men operating from across the water. But the plain fact is that from the very opening of the struggle, American opinion was notably biased in favor of the Allies and against the Central Powers. This can be readily proved by reference to the literature of the time, and it is easily explained. For there is a propaganda of the deed more powerful than any propaganda of the word. It may have been too simple a viewpoint, but what the majority of Americans saw in 1914 was that Austria had declared war on Serbia, that Germany had declared war on Russia, that, in flagrant disregard of a solemn and long-standing treaty three quarters of a century old, the Germans had invaded neutral Belgium. The actions just described gave a bias to opinion in the United States. The British propaganda, which got under way some time later, confirmed and strengthened existing tendencies of thought, rather than created them. Men in general believe what they are predisposed to believe. Sympathy with the democratic nations in 1914 was normal and natural for Americans, and needs no elaborate explanation and no theory of diabolic cunning to make it comprehensible. That the British engaged in propaganda in the United States is true. Propaganda, after all, is the offensive word we apply to the educational activities of others. But it does not follow, because the British made an organized effort to present their side of the war in the United States, that the American people were gulled or duped into believing something they did not wish to believe. On the contrary, they had formed their opinion long before the organized effort got under way. The drift of opinion was clearly indicated in an article in the *Literary Digest* appearing under date of November 14, 1914; it is confirmed by the expression of opinion of many of the leading personalities in the country, such as Theodore Roosevelt and Charles William Eliot.

Or take again the argument that the munitions trade was responsible for our entry into the war. The issue on which America went to war, it must be repeated, was that of the submarine warfare. This issue began to be drawn with the "strict accountability" note of February 10, 1915. It would be impossible to prove that in taking the position which he then took the President was affected either directly or indirectly by men who, two years before it happened, were plotting to involve the United States in war for the sake of profits. Is it likely that Woodrow Wilson with his academic background, his dislike of commercial greed, would be so influenced?

And does not the same line of reasoning apply to the allegation that America went to war to protect its credits? Once again, the issue of the submarine warfare was clearly drawn in the winter and the early spring of 1915. It was outlined before the flow of credit had become significant, and months before the first important war loan to the Allies. And once again, has there been any President of the United States who was less likely to think in purely financial terms, to go to war for purely material reasons, than was Woodrow Wilson? The answer to this question ought not to be difficult in any case. But it will become very evident as we pass from these introductory comments on the events of 1914–1917 to a more complete and searching analysis of American policy.

## One-Sided Neutrality

We start, then, from the proposition that the submarine warfare was the occasion of our entry into the war against the

Reich. But how did that issue develop? And why was it treated in such a manner as to lead to war? This is the fundamental question of the years 1914–1917.

When the war broke out in August of 1914, there can be little question that most Americans, with very rare exceptions, expected the United States to keep out of the struggle. A long tradition suggested that the first reaction to a European war was neutrality; from as far back as Washington's famous Neutrality Proclamation of April, 1793, the precedents pointed to such a course. When, on the sixth of August, President Wilson issued a declaration of similar import, his action was generally approved. It was normal; it was natural; it was in line with past observance. But the President went further than to lay down a general principle of action; he proceeded to supplement it by a second pronouncement, dated August 19, 1914. Impressed, no doubt, by the danger of internal division on the issues of the war, along lines of national origin, he urged the people of the United States to be "neutral in thought as well as in action."

This appeal, however, was from the first a perfectly futile gesture. It was never heeded by the American people, who, as has already been said, in many instances made up their minds early in the struggle as to whom they desired to see the victor. Nor was it really followed out in practice by Wilson or his advisers. From the very outset the President, and for the most part the men closest to him, were decidedly pro-Ally in their feelings. In the case of the President, this is not difficult to understand. Woodrow Wilson was of Scotch-Irish blood; he had early imbibed a great respect for British parliamentary institutions; one of the first and most distinguished of his works had compared the American and British legislatures to the disadvantage of the former; his political thought was steeped in Burke, the greatest British political philosopher of the eighteenth century, and in Bagehot, the greatest British political philosopher of the nineteenth; in the field of literature the English Lake Poets especially commanded his enthusiasm; of the countries of Europe Britain was the only one which he had visited for any length of time, and which he can be said in any real measure to have appreciated. On the other hand, Wilson early showed a great distrust of German militarism. Strongly pacific in his general feeling, so far as international affairs were concerned, opposed to great armed establishments at home or abroad, the President viewed with far from a detached standpoint the onward march of the troops of the Emperor Wilhelm. As early as August 30, 1914, we find him declaring to his friend and confidant, Colonel House, that "if Germany won it would change the course of our civilization, and make the United States a military nation." Still more remarkable is a conversation with Cecil Spring Rice, the British Ambassador at Washington, a few days later. "The President said in the most solemn way," reported the British Minister, "that if the German cause succeeds in the present struggle the United States would have to give up its present ideals and devote all its energies to defense, which would mean the end of its present system of government. He is a great student of Wordsworth, and when I alluded to the sonnets at the time of the great war, especially, 'It is not to be thought of that the flood,' and 'We must be free or die who speak the tongue,'—he said that he knew them by heart, and had them in his mind all the time. I said, 'You and Grey are fed on the same food and I think you understand.' There were tears in his eyes, and I am sure we can, at the right moment, depend on an understanding heart here."

What was true of Wilson was true also of his most intimate friend and closest adviser, Colonel Edward M. House. In 1912 House had written a fanciful romance under the title of

*Philip Dru, Administrator,* which proposed, as the culmination of a long series of domestic reforms, the formation of an international league of peace, based on the co-operation of the United States and Great Britain. House, even more than Wilson, knew England well and loved it; he may even have flattered himself in the summer of 1914 that he had done much to form the mind of his friend along the lines that have just been mentioned.

Mr. Bryan, the Secretary of State, was far less partial to the British, but Mr. Bryan was, of course, totally inexperienced in international affairs; and the most influential personality in the State Department, beyond all question, was the Counselor of the Department, Robert Lansing. Of Mr. Lansing's bias, as of that of Wilson and House, there cannot be the slightest question. Conventional, somewhat legalistic in his viewpoint, he was early to demonstrate the direction of his thinking in the advice which he tendered to his chiefs. As time went on, moreover, his prejudices deepened, and in his *Memoirs* he definitely states that he was by the summer of 1915 convinced that the United States should enter the war if there was any likelihood that Germany would be the victor.

From the outset of the European struggle, then, it was clear that President Wilson and his advisers, to say nothing of the majority of the American people, did not weigh the two sets of the belligerents in the same scales. If one wishes to bewail this fact, one may do so; but it would be more practical and more realistic to accept it as the demonstration of a general principle. For the plain truth is that neutrality, in the sense of perfect impartiality, of complete indifference, has never been possible in periods of general European conflict. It had not been possible in the wars of the French Revolution; at that time the partisanship of the friends of France and that of the friends of England were alike extreme. It had not been possible in the Napoleonic Wars; there existed then the greatest intensity of feeling for and against Britain, an intensity so great in New England when the War of 1812 broke out that there were many men who thoroughly resented and decried our entry into the conflict. It was the same with the revolutionary outbreaks of the middle of the century; Americans had their strong sympathies and their prejudices. They applauded the fall of the Orléans monarchy; they went mad over Kossuth, the Hungarian patriot. *To expect the people of the United States to view the greatest of European events without emotion, without moral judgment, without bias, is to expect from them more than they are capable of. And to understand this is to understand something central in the history of American diplomacy. American neutrality in 1914 was, and had to be, somewhat one-sided; and in their view of the problems of neutrality Woodrow Wilson and his advisers were in accord with the majority opinion of the nation.*

## One-Sided Neutrality in Practice

Having stated the general principle, let us examine the manner in which matters developed in practice. In the fall of 1914, it should be frankly admitted, the administration was certainly quite complacent in its attitude towards British interference with American trade on the high seas. When a rather vigorous protest against certain British practices was drawn up in the State Department towards the end of September, 1914, Wilson and House first toned down the document in question, and then instructed Walter Hines Page, our minister in London, to communicate only its substance. At the same time House held an interview with Cecil Spring-Rice which may well have operated to diminish the effect of the American protest. A little later, a still more remarkable incident occurred. The United States had been requesting of Great Britain that it observe the rules of the Declaration of London, a code of rights and duties of belligerents which had been drawn up five years before, but which had never been accepted by the British government. When the Foreign Office balked at this suggestion, Mr. Lansing, with the approval of the President, drew up a despatch in which he suggested to Sir Edward Grey, the British Foreign Secretary, a means of accepting the Declaration, and then of amending it in such a fashion as to leave Britain's practical position almost unchanged! This remarkable maneuver was not well received in London, and the American government was obliged in due course to give up its insistence upon the Declaration, and fall back upon the general principles of international law; but its action clearly showed that the representations of the United States were for the record rather than an indication of a determined will to challenge the British pretensions on the sea. Other incidents in the fall of the year confirmed this view. When, early in November, on doubtful legal grounds, the British mined the waters of the North Sea, the American government declined to join in a protest which was suggested by one of the Scandinavian states. And at the end of the year, when the State Department sent a new diplomatic note to Great Britain complaining of some of its practices on the high seas, it weakened its own case by suggesting that belligerent interference with neutral trade was justified when it was "manifestly an imperative necessity," and by admitting that belligerent action might rest upon the broad principle of "self-preservation." Clearly the administration was anxious to avoid a sharp challenge to Great Britain.

As the sea war became sharper, it was natural that the German government should seek to retaliate against its enemy. On the fourth of February, 1915, it announced that it would inaugurate two weeks from that date a submarine campaign against all enemy shipping which might approach the British Isles; and though it did not explicitly propose to sink neutral vessels also, it gave warning that these vessels might not be precisely safe if they entered the zone marked out for hostile action. The administration responded to the new German policy very differently from the way it had responded to the British interference with American trade. It lodged a sharp protest on February 10, a protest which asserted the principle that a belligerent had no right whatsoever to sink any vessel, neutral or belligerent, "without first certainly determining its belligerent nationality and the character of its cargo," and which contained as well the ominous sentence that the Government of the United States would be constrained to hold the Imperial German Government to a "strict accountability" for such acts of their naval authorities as violated neutral rights, "and to take any steps it might be necessary to take to safeguard American lives and property and to secure to American citizens the full enjoyment of their acknowledged rights on the high seas."

The note of the tenth of February was certainly framed in a spirit far more rigid and unyielding than had been the various notes to Great Britain. In part this was due to the shock that the German declaration on the U-boat warfare had caused to American opinion. It is difficult for the generation of today, habituated to the carrying on of a warfare that falls hard on noncombatants, to understand the strong feeling aroused by the German action. For centuries merchant vessels had been secure from destruction on the high seas, except in highly special circumstances; and their ruthless destruction, as proposed by Berlin, was a breach with the past that awakened nothing less than horror. The position assumed by the United States had been taken only after consultation with the specially constituted body of experts known as the

Neutrality Board, and it seemed to many persons sound enough in law. But it derived some of its force from the dislike of Germany in general, and perhaps could not have been maintained if that dislike had not existed. Had the political atmosphere been somewhat different, it would not have been difficult to argue that the Reich had been provoked into this measure of retaliation, and that in any case it was unreasonable to jeopardize the neutral position of the United States by insistence upon its rights under international law.

The note of February 10 made no clear distinction between the sinking of *American* merchant ships and the loss of American lives on merchant ships of *belligerent* nationality. Its language would not absolutely have prevented differentiating the one case from the other. But on the twenty-eighth of March, 1915, the life of an American seaman named Thrasher was sacrificed when a German submarine torpedoed the British freighter *Falaba,* and the question now arose in concrete form as to whether or not Germany should be held to the very strictest letter of the law. The debate on this point was sharp. Mr. Bryan, who had signed the protest of February, now brought forward the argument that no American had a right to take passage on a belligerent merchant vessel, and that if he did so he undertook risks for which his government should not be held responsible. He pressed this point with ardor and deep sincerity. Mr. Lansing, on the other hand, took a very different view. An American citizen embarking upon a British ship, he maintained, had a right "to rely upon an enemy's war vessel conforming to the established rules of visit and search and of protection of non-combatants." The President himself, from the beginning, leaned to the second of these two views. But as late as April 23, almost a month after the death of Thrasher, he had not come to a final decision. Before he was to do so, new incidents operated to arouse

American opinion and create a situation in which complacent acceptance of submarine warfare was to become impossible. On May 1 the American steamer *Gulflight* was torpedoed. Six days later, the giant liner *Lusitania* went down beneath the waves off the coast of Ireland, with the loss of over one hundred American lives.

The sinking of the *Lusitania* was not the result of specific instructions from the German Admiralty. On the contrary, it was only by chance that it occurred, and the submarine commander who was responsible for this disaster was himself shocked to see the vessel sink so soon after he had fired his torpedo. But no single act of the war operated more effectively to confirm American hostility to Germany. The press was almost unanimous in condemnation. The President himself was deeply moved. He practiced, it is true, the restraint that was natural to him. In Philadelphia, on the tenth of May, he made his famous speech in which he declared that there was such a thing as a country "being too proud to fight." He desired ardently to keep the nation out of war; of this there can be no doubt. But that a protest should go to Germany, that reparation should be demanded, that the submarine campaign itself should be challenged, were now almost inevitable.

The legal case against the action of the German government was a strong one; but the moral case was stronger still.[1] No

[1] The apologists for the sinking of the *Lusitania* declared that the vessel was armed, that it carried contraband, that it was incorporated in the British Royal Navy, that instructions had been issued by the Admiralty to merchant vessels to ram submarines, that a warning had been published by the German Embassy against American travel on belligerent merchant ships. To this it might be answered: (1) the *Lusitania* was *not* armed; (2) the nature of the cargo does not exempt a belligerent from the duty of visit and search of a merchant vessel; (3) the vessel was not a ship of war, in any sense; (4) the vessel had engaged in no act of hostility; (5) a warning that an illegal act is to be committed does not alter the character of the act.

great and powerful nation would have been likely, in 1915 or at any other time, to see the lives of a hundred of its citizens destroyed by an act altogether without precedent without requiring atonement.

On the thirteenth of May President Wilson launched the first of the notes in which he demanded of Germany disavowal and reparation for the loss of American life on the *Lusitania,* and made it clear that the United States would maintain the "indisputable rights" of its citizens.

The position that Wilson then took was never substantially changed. It was one which meant war if Germany persisted in the U-boat campaign. There were occasions during the next two years when it might have been possible to modify, without abandoning, this position. In July of 1915, for example, the German government proposed that a certain number of neutral vessels, on which Americans might travel, be given safe passage to the British Isles. In September of 1915, as a result of new controversies and sinkings, the Germans gave assurance that "liners" would not be sunk without warning; they were even ready to discuss reparation for the loss of American life on the *Lusitania,* if the United States would waive the question of legal responsibility. But the administration was at all times loyal to principle; it would not abate a jot or a tittle of what it considered American rights.

The most dramatic illustration of this fact came in the famous armed-ship controversy of the winter of 1916. In the submarine controversy as it first developed, the issue turned on the treatment to be accorded unarmed merchant vessels of the belligerents, and on the right of the American to travel upon such ships. But what of *armed* vessels? Did American citizens have a right to travel on the *armed* merchant ships of the Allies? The question became acute in the early spring of 1916 when, seeking for the widest freedom of action possible, hoping for a way out of its troubles with the United States, and encouraged by an ill-judged proposal of Secretary Lansing which had the President's specific sanction, the German government gave warning through a memorandum transmitted to Ambassador Gerard that it intended to sink armed merchant vessels without warning. This warning became known in the United States and led to a serious political crisis. In Congress there was substantial sentiment for accepting the German view. A Texan representative, Jeff McLemore, on the seventeenth of February introduced a resolution warning Americans off such vessels; a tense situation resulted. But the President acted with the greatest vigor. Advised by Secretary Lansing that under the principles of international law merchant vessels had a right to carry defensive armament, and that it was not possible to alter the rules of the game in the midst of war, the President demanded that the McLemore resolution be brought out of committee, and decisively defeated. Though a parliamentary tangle makes it difficult to interpret with complete confidence the vote that resulted, there can be no question that Wilson's attitude prevailed in practice, and that the Congressional movement aimed at concession to Germany was effectively and decisively scotched.

A later generation of historical writers has been exceedingly critical of the President's unyielding attitude in the armed-ship controversy. The validity of the legal position assumed has been sharply questioned by authorities of the very highest rank, and it is putting the matter very moderately to say that the matter was debatable. That Wilson judged severely and not without feeling where Germany was concerned should be admitted. But one fact with regard to his judgment must be kept in mind. It was in tune, on the whole, with the judgment of the American people. The "strict accountability" note of February 10th had met with almost no criticism from the press. The sinking of the *Lusitania* was condemned by most of the influential newspapers. There was a very remarkable unanimity of judgment, so far as editorial comment was concerned, behind the President's stand against the McLemore resolution. Let us admit that we do not have the data for a truly scientific and authoritative study of American public opinion in 1915 and 1916. It still remains true, from what evidence one can gather, that the country was, by and large, behind the President. His rigidity of viewpoint reflected the rising public feeling against Germany.

It was not, however, the submarine warfare alone that was responsible for this feeling. There were other matters that tended to influence the American mind. In the early fall of 1915, for example, the *New York World* had published an exposé of German underground activities in the United States which, though it revealed nothing very hair-raising, undoubtedly contributed to the drift of public sentiment. In September, it was discovered that the Austrian Minister, Dr. Dumba, had looked with favor upon a plan to incite strikes in munitions plants, and his recall was requested. At about the same time German sympathizers were arrested on the charge of planning to destroy merchant ships with cargoes of arms, and these men were shown to be amply supplied with funds from some unknown source. The German military and naval attachés, the notorious Von Papen and the less notorious Boy-Ed, were apparently engaged in illegal activities, and in November they followed Dr. Dumba on the route of recall. A great wave of agitation in favor of national preparedness was sweeping the country.

American hostility to the Reich was undeniably growing. It is useless, and would indeed be quite unjust and inaccurate, to assume that President Wilson was acting independently of public opinion in 1916, or dragging the country forward along a course which it had no desire to follow.

For a time, moreover, it seemed as if his policy were to be successful. In the spring of 1916, an unarmed merchant vessel, the *Sussex,* was torpedoed in the English Channel, and some Americans were injured. Wilson now demanded the complete abandonment of the submarine warfare, on threat of severance of relations with Germany. The threat was effective. The German government yielded. True, it accompanied its action with the declaration that its decision was conditional on the administration's ability to secure from Great Britain respect for American rights on the seas. But the President ignored the condition; and from the spring of 1916 to the winter of 1917 the issue of the U-boats sank into the background. For the time being the President had kept us out of war.

## The Diplomacy of 1916

The events and the diplomacy of 1916 illustrate the innate pacific temper of the people of the United States. In the perspective of 1944, there will be some who will say that the issues of twenty-five years ago were much larger than those of the submarine warfare, that in putting the case against Germany on this restricted legal ground the President was ignoring the larger aspects of the struggle, of which he spoke in private, and that cardinal American interests were involved in the defeat of a power whose ambition and ruthlessness are the wonder of the world today. Perhaps there is force in this view. But the American people certainly did not perceive it, then; it was not often stated even by the partisans of the Allies; and it seems fair to say that Germany would, in all probability, have succeeded in avoiding a conflict with the United States if she had remained faithful to her assurances of the spring of 1916. The course of the next few months was marked by a coolness in American feeling, and in the attitude of the administration, towards Great Britain; it was also marked by the revival of a long-cherished hope in administration circles that it might be possible for the United States to bring about peace between the contending belligerents.

As to the first of these matters, the change in sentiment towards Britain, it is to be noted that in the late spring and early summer of 1916 causes of substantial irritation arose against the government in London. The Irish rebellion of April had aroused much antagonism in the United States—not wholly among British Americans. The British naval authorities had by this time put into effect more and more drastic measures to stop all trade with Germany, measures which were, in the opinion of the American Neutrality Board, distinctly contrary to international law. Public opinion was irked by the dilatoriness and evasiveness of the Foreign Office in answering American protests. Interference with the mails was particularly annoying, and so, too, was the publication of a British black list of American firms suspected of doing business with Germany. Resentment against such practices was felt not only in the White House, but in Congress. The passage of the great naval bill of 1916 was as much a challenge to Britain as to Germany. Equally important was the enactment of two laws which gave the President authority to take retaliatory measures against Britain, even to the extent of denying clearance papers to any ship unfairly discriminating against the commerce of American citizens, and refusing port facilities to the merchant marine of any nation that employed discriminating practices against American trade, and which even made possible the imposition of an embargo upon exports to Britain.

It is worth while insisting on these facts. One can never tell, and one never ought to assert positively, what *would* have happened in history. But if the annoyance with Great Britain had persisted, and the Germans had abstained from troubling, it would at least have been very difficult for this country to have gone to war on the side of the Allies. There was still a strong peace spirit in the United States.

As a matter of fact, in the fall of 1916 President Wilson was seriously considering some move on the part of the United States to bring the war to an end. In the previous winter he had sent Colonel House abroad on a mission, one purpose of which was to explore the possibilities of peace. The mission had been rather futile, but Wilson was now getting ready to try again. It is difficult, however, to make any decisive move in the field of diplomacy in the autumn of a Presidential year. The student of American foreign policy may often remark the paralysis that comes over our government in just such circumstances. At such a time those in authority hesitate to make vital decisions which may cost votes. An administration which may be repudiated in a month or two is a weak administration, almost from the necessity of the case, and is naturally reluctant to start something it cannot finish. They do things better in Great Britain, where the life of a government has been more than once prolonged in a period of crisis and party maneuvers shoved into the background which they ought to occupy in time of war.

After his re-election Wilson did, indeed, make one last effort. In a move that coincided with Berlin's own suggestion of a peace discussion (and that was widely denounced by the more ardent partisans of the Allies on that account), Wilson called upon the two sets of warring powers to state the terms on which they would be willing to end the war. By this time he knew that in Berlin the drift was towards the resumption of the U-boat warfare; indeed, as early as the eleventh of October the Reichstag had voted that the Imperial Chancellor was to "base his attitude with regard to the U-boat question on the conclusion reached by the Supreme High Command."

Wilson's peace move of December, 1916, was not in the least productive. It met with a cool rebuff from Germany which declared that "the most suitable way of arriving at the desired result" was through a "direct exchange of views between the belligerent powers." It was answered by the Allies with more precision, but in such fashion as to make it clear that drastic territorial changes must be made to satisfy the democratic nations, and that only a decisive victory could induce Germany and her allies to concede such changes. As a matter of fact, the Entente and the Central Powers were poles apart at the end of 1916; the hope of peace was an iridescent dream. The Germans were by no means ready to confess defeat, as Bethmann-Hollweg's confidential statement of terms shows; Great Britain and France, as has just been stated, were determined on complete victory.

For Germany, then, there remained the submarine warfare, as one of the last weapons in her armory. The fatal decision was taken on the ninth of January, when the long resistance of the Chancellor, Bethmann-Hollweg, was broken down. The Kaiser also was now ready to go ahead. On January 19th Count von Bernstorff received word of the decision of the Imperial Government. In vain the Ambassador issued the most solemn warnings of the folly of their course to the authorities of Berlin. The most that could be conceded was the telegraphing to Washington of Germany's terms of peace, which would not for one moment have been accepted by the Allies. On the thirty-first of January Bernstorff, ill-at-ease and unhappy, made his last call at the State Department, instructed to give to Mr. Lansing word of the German decision. On the third of February relations were formally broken off with Germany.

Even now President Wilson was reluctant to make the ultimate decision for war. On the twenty-sixth of February he requested authority to arm the merchant ships of the United

States. When the measure to give him this authority failed in the last days of the session, he decided that he could act alone, and did so on the twelfth of March. On the fourteenth came the sinking of the American steamship, the *Algonquin*. By the twentieth of March the cabinet was unanimous for war; and influenced by this fact, no doubt, the President summoned the new Congress for two weeks earlier than he had originally intended, for the second of April. On that day he delivered his famous war message, and in the few days following Congress acted upon his recommendation. The Senate voted for war by a vote of 82 to 6; in the House there was a more substantial opposition, and the vote was 373 to 50.

In reviewing the events of the end of 1916 and 1917, we see once again that the submarine holds the center of the stage. It would be absurd to suggest, of course, that no other considerations justifying American entry into the struggle could possibly have occurred to anyone. There must have been Americans by this time, for example, who thought of the stake which the great loans made to the Allies gave the United States in Allied victory; there must have been Americans who saw in the Russian revolution of mid-March an additional reason for participation in the war, both because that revolution destroyed the only autocracy on the side of the Entente nations, and because it made the chance of victory without our aid more doubtful. There must, indeed, have been all sorts of interpretations of what was actually to occur. But the fact remains that without the submarine warfare it is very doubtful whether war would have come.

The best evidence of this lies in the circumstances surrounding President Wilson's re-election. He had won in a very close contest. And the slogan which had done much to re-elect him, which had carried for him almost every state west of the Mississippi, was the slogan, "He kept us out of war." The

President, it is true, had made no promises for the future. He had, indeed, warned of the danger that he might not be able to continue his pacific policy. But he was judged by what he had already accomplished, and to many persons he appeared to have brought Germany to terms without resort to force. There was a strong peace sentiment, in other words, behind his victory.

By their reassumption of the submarine warfare, the Germans dissipated much, perhaps most, of this sentiment in a matter of weeks. They, and no one else, were responsible for the final decision. They chose to challenge the United States. They unified American opinion, and made American participation in the world struggle inevitable.

## Summary

*There are still those, no doubt, who are critical of the Wilsonian diplomacy of 1914–1917. A more scrupulous and more evenly balanced neutrality, these persons would maintain, might have prevented the involving of the United States in the First World War. But to say this is to be completely unrealistic. The American people are not likely to be impartial in a world conflict; the administration that represents them is not likely to be. They are bound to be influenced by their prejudices, their ideals, their hopes. They were so influenced thirty years ago.*

*But there is more than this to be said. Though Wilson placed the case against Germany, throughout the period of neutrality, on narrow legal grounds, though he may have been unwise in doing so, as we look at the matter today we may well contend that there was more than legality at stake. Facing the menace of National Socialism in 1944, does it not seem reasonable to contend that in opposing the growth of German power, and forestalling the menace of German victory,*

*Woodrow Wilson acted in the national interest? His intervention may well have prevented the collapse of Britain. There was a time in 1917 when no less a person than Lord Jellicoe actually stated that if matters did not change for the better Britain could not hold out six weeks. Would the collapse of Britain have been of no concern to America? Would a shift in the balance of power that gave free scope to German ambition have been a matter of no concern? Would neutrality, if it meant German victory, have been to the interest of the United States? It is doubtful if many Americans would answer that question with a "Yes" today.*

III

# The Diplomacy of the War Years, 1917–1918

*The occasion of the war with Germany, 1917–1918, was the submarine warfare. But the objectives, as shaped by Woodrow Wilson, were the establishment of a League of Peace, the attainment of security, the overthrow of German militarism, the redrawing of the map of Europe on a "just" basis. The way seemed to be paved for these objectives by the armistice of November 11, 1918. But, in retrospect, the overthrow of the Imperial régime was an ineffective guarantee of peace; the negotiations which led up to the armistice permitted the German people to believe that they had been duped into capitulation, not conquered in the field.*

*The diplomacy of the war years 1917–1918 is interesting and important to the student of American foreign policy from a variety of standpoints. It illustrates in the first place how, once war comes, the issues involved broaden and deepen—perhaps inevitably; it raises questions of policy that are important from the angle of our own day; and it provides some interesting comparisons and contrasts with the diplomacy of 1941–1944.*

## The Objectives of American Diplomacy

The occasion of the war into which the United States entered on April 7, 1917, was the submarine warfare. Without that direct challenge from Germany, it is doubtful if peace-loving America, whatever its partiality for the Allies, would have actually entered the conflict. But a war for neutral rights seems and then seemed a war for very limited objects. It was necessary to give to the struggle a larger meaning. This is what President Wilson attempted to do in his great war address of April 2, 1917, and in his subsequent utterances.

### (*A*) *A League of Peace*

In the first place, he set for himself and the nation which he led a very large and very high objective, one that would challenge the idealism and stimulate the hopes of the American people. This was nothing less than an association of nations which would make the recurrence of a World War impossible; nothing less, to use the President's own eloquent words, than a "universal dominion of right by such a concert of free peoples as shall bring peace and safety to all nations, and make the world itself at last free"—in other words, the development of a League of Nations. The idea, as Wilson propounded it in the speech of April 2, was not, of course, new—not even new to him.

An American branch of the League to Enforce Peace, a private organization which advocated the idea of collective action against aggressor nations, was organized under the Presidency of William Howard Taft in the spring of 1915. At the same time similar discussions were going on in England. Sir Edward Grey, the British Foreign Secretary, began to take a keen interest in the matter; indeed as early as February, 1915, he had suggested to Colonel House that the United States ought to "come into some general guarantee of world-wide peace." He reiterated the same idea to the Colonel in August, and again in September. By these channels the idea of a League of Peace was forcibly brought to the attention of President Wilson. In November, Wilson permitted his confidant to indicate to Grey his general sympathy with the broad conception of a concert of nations bound together to prevent war. Early in the next year he made his first public commitment. In one of his preparedness speeches, at Des Moines, he definitely expressed the hope that the war would end in the formation of "some sort of joint guarantee of peace on the part of the great nations of the world." Nearly four months later came the memorable pronouncement at a dinner of the League to Enforce Peace in Washington that the United States was "ready to become a partner in any feasible association of nations" formed to prevent aggression and protect the rights and liberties of small nations. When the Democratic nominating convention met in June of 1916, Wilson saw to it that there was inserted in the party platform a declaration in favor of a "feasible association" of nations. In the course of the Presidential campaign which followed, Wilson underlined the League idea again and again. The speech of April 2 was a solemn commitment to a purpose long since declared.

## (*B*) *Security*

But there was a second aspect to Wilson's interpretation of the war that needs to be carefully considered. The President believed that the European war involved the safety and the security of the United States. We have already seen that in his conversations with Colonel House and with Cecil Spring-Rice, the President had declared that a German victory would jeopardize the peaceful world order in which America had grown to maturity. His conception of neutrality, his eagerness to bring about peace between the belligerents, had prevented him from expressing this opinion in public. But in the war address of April 2 he stated it and stated it in unforgettable language, in the famous phrase, "The world must be made safe for democracy." This phrase has been often misquoted, and widely misunderstood. Wilson did not say that every state must become democratic (though he may have thought so).

He said that the democratic order must be *made safe*. By this he meant that if Europe became militarized, and fell under German domination, it would be necessary for the rest of the world to follow in its train, and that in the course of this process popular institutions themselves would be placed in jeopardy. "We are accepting this challenge of hostile purpose," he declared in another part of the speech of April 2, "because we know that in such a government . . . we can never have a friend; and that in the presence of its organized power, always lying in wait to accomplish we know not what purpose, there can be no assured security for the democratic governments of the world." This opinion he more than once repeated in his later war utterances. In May, for example, he spoke of the Reich as having linked together government after government in "a net of intrigue directed against nothing less than the peace and liberties of the world." In June, in his Flag Day Address, he put the matter still more unequivocally. If the rulers of Germany succeed, he declared, "America will fall within the menace. We and all the rest of the world must remain armed, as they will remain, and must make ready for the next step in their aggression; if they fail, the world may unite for peace." Two months later, he described the situation in language even stronger, declaring that the object of the war was to "deliver the free peoples of the world from the menace and actual power of a vast military establishment, controlled by an irresponsible government" which had "secretly planned to dominate the world."

How far views such as these just quoted were held by the American people it is impossible to say, without a prolonged study of the newspapers and public addresses of the time. It is curious how little of this emphasis is to be found in the debates on the war declaration in Congress, or even in the speeches of such strong partisans of the Allies as Theodore

Roosevelt and James M. Beck. The best, the clearest, and as it appears today the most farsighted statement in support of the doctrine of security came from Mr. Walter Lippmann, then connected with the *New Republic*. Mr. Lippmann, in the pages of that magazine, went far beyond the thought of the President. He declared then, as he has declared in our own time, that when Germany "burst into the Atlantic" the United States was compelled to go to war, not for any abstract reason, but from the sheer instinct of self-preservation. The peace of the nineteenth century, he stated with much cogency, rested upon the fact that the dominant power of the period was Great Britain, and upon the moderate use which she made of her power. The defeat of Britain, and of her Western ally, would have jeopardized an international order under which America had grown great, and in which she had an interest which might be described as an interest of self-preservation.

It is not hard for the thought of our own time to accept, or at any rate to regard with great respect, this interpretation of the war of 1917. No one, of course, can say with certainty what would have happened if events had not been what they were. But is it very hard to believe today that a German victory a quarter of a century ago would have been the prelude to new acts of ambition and power on the part of the victorious Reich?

### (C) *The Overthrow of Kaiserism*

There is another respect, however, in which the Wilsonian point of view in 1917 seems less acceptable to the Americans of 1944. In his speech of April 2, and many times thereafter, Wilson drew a distinction between the German government and the German people. The one was guilty; the other relatively innocent. The one must be overthrown; the other might be treated with charity. There is no question that the President believed in this distinction. More fully than the facts of history warrant, he upheld the view that the peoples of the world were pacific, that only wicked and designing statesmen and generals were responsible for war. He was to embroider this theme again and again in the public utterances of 1917, to stress the fact that the war was brought about by a small political and military oligarchy, not by the body of the German nation. Implicit in what he had to say was the proposition that a change of government in the Reich was necessary to future peace. The position which he took meant that one of the objectives of the war would be the overthrow of the Imperial régime and the establishment of a German republic upon its ruins.

That Wilson was right in making the distinction between the rulers of Germany and the German people may well be doubted. But whether his thesis was sound or not, it was certainly useful. It induced and was meant to induce a tolerant attitude toward the many Americans of German origins within the boundaries of the United States. It did more than this. It operated to separate the rulers from the ruled in the Reich, and in due course to help produce the revolution that came with the ending of the war.

## (D) *A Just Territorial Settlement*

A League to preserve the peace, American security, the overthrow of a wicked government, these became the proclaimed objectives of the United States. But to these one more objective had to be added. If not at the outset, certainly within two months of our entry into the conflict, the United States was committed to important territorial changes on the other side of the Atlantic. How did this come about, and what did it imply?

It had been for a long time the thesis of the President, in the days of neutrality, that the United States could not and would not be concerned with the actual terms of peace, but only with the bringing about of that happy consummation. However, as Wilson began to attach more and more importance to the idea of a League of Nations, he began to feel that the nature of the European settlement was highly important, that on it might hinge American adhesion to the League itself. This idea was hardly hinted at in the speech to the League to Enforce Peace on May 27, 1916; but it was clearly brought out in the so-called "peace without victory" address, delivered before the Senate just before American entry into the war. "The terms of the immediate peace agreed upon," the President declared, "will determine whether it is a peace for which . . . a guarantee can be secured." But what would just terms be? It was some time before the President went further. He was compelled to do so by the agitation which began in 1917 for a settlement based upon the principle of "no annexation and no indemnities." This seductive formula, wherever it originated, exercised a great attraction upon the Russians, who, war-weary and torn with revolution, were weakening in their determination to carry the war through to a completely victorious conclusion. It was exploited to the full in Germany; in July of 1917 the German Reichstag formally adopted it in a famous resolution. To Wilson, however, it seemed to imperil the objectives of the war itself. "It was the status quo ante out of which this iniquitous war issued forth," he declared in a message to Russia, dated May 26, 1917; "that status must be altered in such fashion as to prevent any such hideous thing from happening again. Practical questions can be settled only by practical means. Phrases will not accomplish the result. Effective readjustments will; and whatever readjustments are necessary must be made." In such language, less than two months after American entry into the war, the President committed himself to territorial readjustments at its close.

What should those readjustments be? The question became increasingly urgent as the first year of war flowed on. For in Russia matters were going from bad to worse; in November occurred the revolution which brought the Bolsheviks into power; and one of the first moves of this new government was to propose an armistice for the discussion of terms of peace. In England and in the United States there was a growing clamor in circles describing themselves as "liberal" for the clearer definition of objectives, for a positive program. As early as September there had been constituted in this country the "Inquiry," a carefully chosen body of experts, to study and report upon the complex territorial questions which would call for settlement at the end of the war. With the materials which this body had collected to serve as a guide, the President, on the eighth of January, 1918, delivered the famous speech which is known to history as the Speech of the Fourteen Points, which was nothing less than a program, "the only possible program," as Wilson stated it, for the termination of the war.

I shall not examine the fourteen points item by item, detail by detail. They were not so precise as not to leave some room for maneuver and negotiation. But they suggested, if they did not guarantee, far-reaching changes (such, for example, as the return of Alsace-Lorraine to France) in which only a beaten nation could acquiesce. And, what was still more important, they seemed to say that the United States must play a part in drawing the new map of Europe. They did more. They implied that the peace at the end of the war must be a "just" peace, that it must be based upon the principle of self-determination, upon the right of the peoples of the world to determine their own destiny. They meant, inevitably, that at the end of the war the President must contend for a settlement in accordance with his professed ideals. They foreshadowed the struggle of 1919 in Paris.

That struggle is, of course, to be treated in a later chapter. But with regard to it, one thing ought to be said here. In the Speech of the Fourteen Points, and in some of his subsequent addresses, the President spoke as if there were possible a settlement that met some universal standard of justice. That idea was to be proved incorrect. In the complex boundary problems of Europe, be it understood thus early in the story, there is often no answer that would be accepted by all parties as reasonable and right. To hold out hopes of such an answer was to offer more than could be attained. It was to pave the way for a disillusionment at the end of the war that was neither healthy in itself nor favorable to the maintenance of the peace that had been made.

## The Secret Treaties

Before we leave the Speech of the Fourteen Points and the question of territorial readjustments at the end of the war, we must go back for a little to speak of the secret treaties, the relation to them of this most famous of Wilson's utterances, and of the criticism, often uttered, that Wilson was the dupe of wicked European diplomats from the very outset of the struggle. That such treaties existed was, of course, true. The governments which were contending against Germany had appetites to satisfy, as well as aspirations to be realized; the Italians, for example, had been promised large additions of territory as the price of their entry into the war; France had made an agreement with Russia by which the left bank of the Rhine was to be detached from Germany; Russia had been promised Constantinople and the freedom of the Straits; Rumania had been induced to enter the war by the promise of Transylvania; the German colonies and the vast reaches of the Ottoman Empire in Asia had been the subject of special understandings. The government of the United States was committed to none of these objectives; but had she by the force of circumstances been made an unwilling partner to their realization?

So it has seemed to some of the critics of Woodrow Wilson; and with the wisdom that comes from hindsight these individuals have sometimes said that as a very condition of our entry into the war the secret treaties should have been revised. The suggestion appears to me to be based upon a misconception. Though the President had some knowledge of the Treaty of London, he was certainly not aware of all these engagements when we entered the war; and of some of them he only learned at the time of the peace conference in Paris. But suppose he *had* known of them. How could he have demanded a price for taking the action which he believed to be necessary to vindicate American rights and American honor; and if he had demanded it, is it at all certain that the bargain would have been kept? It seems a little naïve to believe so.

Wilson chose another and wiser line of action. He set forth his own purposes and the purposes of the United States explicitly in the Speech of the Fourteen Points; and then he sought, as we shall see, to get these purposes accepted by the Allies in the armistice negotiations of 1918. He succeeded. He could rightfully claim, in the peace negotiations of 1919, that the victorious nations of Europe were bound by the principles he had laid down, and that the secret treaties, where they were in conflict with those principles, had been superseded.

## The United States and the Orient, 1917–1918

In discussing the views and purposes of the American government in 1917, there is a final point to be stressed. Wilson wished, very naturally, to give to the struggle the character of a great crusade against wrongdoing, to make it as universal as possible. There were certain difficulties in the way of such a course. In the Orient, for example, the situation was highly unfavorable to American diplomacy.

The World War had been an invitation to Japan to inaugurate the policy of encroachment in China which was, a quarter of a century later, to lead to a direct clash with the United States. Already installed in Manchuria, as a result of the Russo-Japanese War, Japan had taken advantage of the outbreak of the European struggle to enter the war on the side of the Allies and seize the German leasehold of Kiaochow. Less than a year later, in the spring of 1915, she had proposed to the weak government of the Chinese Republic the famous Twenty-one Demands, which, if accepted in their entirety, would have virtually established a Japanese protectorate over that state. Confronted with resistance—and embarrassing publicity—Tokyo had been obliged to modify its position; but it came out of the discussions, nonetheless, with very concrete gains, and with agreement which virtually transformed the great province of Shantung (in which Kiaochow was situated) into a Japanese sphere of influence.

The United States had been compelled to acquiesce in these events; occupied elsewhere, it had been puzzled as to what course to pursue, and had spoken with an uncertain voice. In March of 1915, Secretary Bryan had gone so far as to admit, in speaking of the Twenty-one Demands, that "territorial contiguity" created "special relations" for Japan not only in South Manchuria and East Mongolia, but in Shantung! Two months later, however, he seemed to regret his action. In May, when informed of the acceptance of the Demands (somewhat modified, it is true), the Secretary put it on record that the United States could not recognize "any agreement or undertaking which has been entered into between the governments of Japan and China, impairing the treaty rights of the United States and its citizens in China or the political and territorial integrity of the Republic of China, or in the international policy relative to China commonly known as the Open Door." Beyond this, however, the American government had not ventured to go. Its purpose, in the Far East, was to keep out of trouble; this was wholly logical in view of the tension in our relations with the Reich, and the policy of caution was still, very naturally, being continued when the United States went to war with Germany in April, 1917.

A power which had to be addressed in such terms was hardly likely to be the warm ally of a warlike America; there was suspicion at both Tokyo and Washington; and just before our entry into the war, the Japanese had thoughtfully negotiated a series of secret treaties with their Allies, which bound the latter to support their claims, not only to Kiaochow, but also to the islands which they had by this time so prudently picked up in the Pacific, and which were to be so useful at a later epoch. Nor was the situation in China in 1917 at all to American liking. The Chinese Republic was torn with strife between militarists and the friends of a constitutional order; its power and its authority were feeble; and though it finally entered the war, in order to have a place at the peace table, its decision added little to the moral weight of the Allied cause.

## The United States and Latin America

If it was difficult to fit the situation in the Orient into the pattern of a great crusade, it was difficult also (though less difficult) with regard to Latin America.

In the years of war, 1917–1918, it can hardly be said that the other states of the Western Hemisphere rallied with one accord to the American standard. The adhesion of certain of these states could, of course, be taken for granted. There could be no doubt about Cuba, or Panama, or, for the most part, the states of Central America, which were in a sense the economic and political clients of the United States. Haiti and the Dominican Republic were under the occupation of our marines, and were hardly free agents. Before the war was far advanced, Brazil gave evidence of her co-operative spirit by a severance of relations with Germany, and on October 26, 1917, after outrages against Brazilian shipping, she declared war. Uruguay made the friendly gesture of declaring that she would not treat the United States as a belligerent, setting a new principle of action in inter-American relations, and her example was followed by Bolivia and Peru. Ecuador went so far as to sever relations with the Reich. But despite all this, six states, four of them very important states, remained strictly neutral. The attitude of little El Salvador or of Paraguay could hardly be expected to arouse much concern at Washington. But it was distinctly unpleasant that Mexico, with regard to which Woodrow Wilson had practised such remarkable forbearance in the revolutionary years from 1913 to 1917, whose Chief of State in part owed his elevation to power to the policy of the American government, should be not only indifferent, but almost hostile. And on the South American Continent it was the larger and more important states, always excepting Brazil, which adopted a position of neutrality. Colombia and Venezuela, Chile and Argentina, these were countries of substantial size and political significance; and not one of them adhered to the American cause. It was not that Woodrow Wilson had not recognized the importance of good relations with the sister republics of the New World. As early as October, 1913, he had sought to win their confidence by his famous declaration at Mobile that the United States would never again seek a foot of territory by conquest. As has been already mentioned, he wished to sponsor a Pan-American pact of mutual guarantees of territorial integrity and political independence. In 1915 a Pan-American Financial Congress had met at Washington to cement the economic relations of the United States with the countries to the south. But all this had been in part counterbalanced by the forcible interventions of the United States in Haiti and the Dominican Republic. In addition, Colombia had an unliquidated grievance based on the hasty recognition by President Roosevelt of the Panamanian Republic in 1903. Mexico was passing through a period of intense nationalism, well typified in its crotchety and sensitively proud executive, General Venustiano Carranza. Argentina was much more closely associated with Europe than with this country by the natural flow of her trade, and then, as later, felt a touch of jealousy as she contemplated the great republic of the North. Chile was remote, and on the whole indifferent. Taking the overall picture, it cannot be said that there existed a true Pan-American solidarity in 1917, or that the states of Latin America rallied with unanimity or intense enthusiasm to the cause of the United States. Events were to fall out more favorably in 1941.

## The Conduct of the War

So much for the objectives, the diplomatic position of the United States in the war of 1917. What steps were taken, as victory drew near, towards the consolidation of these objectives? The question is an important one. Before we answer it, it may be well to understand the fundamental facts with regard to the progress of the war itself.

Americans who slipped into the doldrums in 1942 might well have refreshed themselves by thinking back to twenty-five years before. The submarine warfare, a deadly menace in the spring of 1917 (the Germans sank over 850,000 tons of shipping in April, 1917), was soon, it is true, to be brought under control. In every other respect, the picture was a gloomy one. The French offensive of the spring of 1917 had been bloody and futile, had even led to mutinies among some of the French troops. The summer had seen the collapse of Russian power, after a short-lived offensive. The fall had been marked by the crushing defeat of the Italians at Caporetto; only by a hair had Italy been saved from complete collapse. Then came the Bolshevik revolution; and on its heels the peace negotiations at Brest-Litovsk. True, faced by German ruthlessness and brutality, the Bolshevik leaders hesitated as to taking Russia out of the war. Trotsky, the Minister of Foreign Affairs, made an important inquiry through Raymond Robins, head of the American Red Cross in Russia, as to what assistance the Bolshevik government could expect from the United States if it continued the struggle. But the chances of effective aid to Russia were virtually nil. The British and French governments, especially the latter, viewed the new régime with a deep suspicion which was not allayed when in December the Bolsheviks published the secret treaties, and when in February they repudiated the Russian debts. In any case, the practical difficulties in the way of providing large-scale military co-operation for Russia would have been enormous. The signing of the treaty of Brest-Litovsk, on the third of March, 1918, was one of those disasters which could hardly have been avoided, but which must always be remembered in judging both the diplomacy of the war and the diplomacy of the peace.

What it did, of course, was to permit the Germans to concentrate their forces on the Western Front for one last desperate effort. In the face of this new menace only the most intimate co-operation between the Allies could avert defeat. On the whole, taking into consideration the profound breach with tradition involved in the American participation in the war, the attitude of the Wilson administration deserves the highest praise. From an early period immense advances in funds were made to the hard-pressed Allies, sums without which British and French credit would have collapsed and victory have been impossible. A flood of supplies crossed the Atlantic. Two months after our entry into the war, a conscription act provided for the raising of armies such as had never been seen in American history. In the fall, largely though by no means entirely as a result of American urging, a great inter-Allied conference was held in Paris, with Colonel House heading a distinguished American mission. An understanding was reached as to the use of American military and naval power, and committees constituted to deal with special problems, and to carry out or modify the decisions taken. But the largest question of all remained to be decided. The successful conduct of the war depended, so President Wilson strongly believed, upon the unity of the military command. It was difficult to get the British to accept this view. The Supreme War Council, set up in November, was a body of confused powers and functions, both political and military. It was not until the German offensive at the end of March, 1918, that the pressure of events, and the insistence of the French and the Americans, finally overcame British opposition. The appointment of Marshal Foch as the Generalissimo of the Armies on the Western Front was, in part, a victory for President Wilson, and would have been impossible without his clarity of vision and his willingness to subordinate national jealousies to the great end of common victory. The America of 1917–1918 set a marvelous example for a later generation to imitate when it went as far as it did go towards the articulation of its own war effort with that of the transatlantic democracies. By such united action the way was paved for the great victory of 1918.

It is not necessary, of course, to describe in detail the momentous military operations of this latter year. The German offensive shattered itself against the heroic resistance of the Allied armies; and in July was launched the counteroffensive that was to result in the collapse of German power.

The great Allied attack upon the German lines in the West began in the sector between Soissons and Château-Thierry, with many American troops engaged. On the eighth of August the British launched a terrific blow far to the north; they breached the Hindenburg Line; and even more important than this they met with evidence of war weariness and lowered morale in the German armies which resisted them. These were black days for the German High Command, as Ludendorff was later to confess; and the gloom was not lightened at the war council which took place at Spa on August 14. For in addition to defeat in the field, Germany now faced the collapse of her allies. The Austrian Emperor Charles and his Foreign Secretary, Count Burian, who were present at the conference, made no bones of their opinion that the moment had come to open negotiations with the democracies; from this time forward they exerted a steady pressure in favor of such action, and by mid-September went so far as to launch an independent peace proposal of their own. In Bulgaria and in Turkey the military situation was steadily deteriorating; the Allied army of General Franchet d'Espérey stood poised at Salonika, and before the end of September it was to compel the government at Sofia to sue for peace. The significance of these collateral events on the action of the German military and civil authorities must not be underestimated.

It seems certain that by the end of August the German General Staff, and especially General Ludendorff, recognized that the defeat of the Reich was inevitable. But he and his colleague, von Hindenburg, hesitated to face the facts; for a month they concealed the seriousness of the situation from the Chancellor, von Hertling. And then there came a moment of panic — nothing less. On September 29 the German High Command recommended an immediate appeal to President Wilson. On the first of October its tone became insistent and urgent. "Today the troops are holding their own; what may happen tomorrow cannot be foreseen." So intense was now the feeling that action must be taken immediately that when Hindenburg agreed to a day's delay while a new German government should be formed, Ludendorff asked that the note be sent at once. "They have lost all their nerve, here," wrote the Foreign Office representative at General Headquarters. It was the military authorities, not the newly constituted government of Prince Max of Baden, who would not consider anything less than immediate action in the crisis of Germany's fortunes. It was clearly realized, and clearly stated by the new Chancellor, that peace might well mean the loss of the German colonies, of Alsace-Lorraine, of substantial Polish-speaking districts in Eastern Germany; and it was only after the High Command had declared in writing that there could not be an instant's delay that the first of the series of peace notes which terminated the war was sent to Woodrow Wilson. How far the first step along the road to complete capitulation was due to a nervous collapse on the part of General Ludendorff, how far it is in the nature of the German temperament and of the German military machine thus to lose all sense of proportion when it sees defeat staring it in the face, is a question that must be left to the judgment of the reader.

### The Armistice Negotiations

In the negotiations of October and early November Woodrow Wilson displayed a remarkable realism, a complete sincerity, and a very genuine diplomatic skill. There were many who regarded the German overture to Wilson with the deepest suspicion, and who feared that the President might be duped. The facts were to refute them. In a series of remarkable state papers the President drove the Germans from one position to another, laying a solid basis for the armistice itself. Thus, to Max of Baden's note of October 3, Wilson responded on October 9, demanding the evacuation of Belgium and Northern France as a *sine qua non* of negotiations. At the same time he raised the question as to whether the Chancellor was speaking for the German people, or merely "for the constituted authorities of the Empire who have so far conducted the war." The German note had spoken of the Fourteen Points as "a *basis* of peace negotiations." The American reply demanded that they be accepted explicitly. There was certainly no naïveté and no weakness in this first diplomatic exchange with the Reich.

On October 12, the German government accepted the conditions laid down in the American note of October 9, and proposed "the meeting of a mixed commission for making the necessary arrangements concerning the evacuation." It was evidently hoped that under the guise of a suspension of hostilities, the German armies might be re-formed and re-grouped on their own territory. Again the President took firm and strong ground. On October 14 the Germans were told that the conditions of the armistice "must be left to the advice of the military advisers of the Government of the United States and the Allied Governments." They were also told that the submarine warfare must cease before the way could be open to discussion. And once again it was indicated that the enemies of Germany must be convinced that the power of the militarists had been subordinated to the authority of the German people. In the second skirmish as in the first, Wilson not only held his own ground, but exerted an increasing pressure on the government of the Reich.

The second Wilson note brought the German leaders face to face with the magnitude of their defeat. They were called upon to confess that they were beaten, and they naturally balked at doing so. The leaders of the General Staff, so urgent for negotiations two weeks before, now began to talk of a last-ditch resistance. But the process of demoralization of German opinion had now progressed far; the hopes of peace, once aroused, demanded to be satisfied. The military situation was steadily deteriorating; and on the twentieth the government of Max of Baden decided to yield to the President. In its reply, it made it clear that "in the future no government can take or continue in office without possessing the confidence of the majority of the Reichstag"; it indicated that an amendment to the German Constitution had been introduced which would vest decisions of peace and war solely in the people; it declared that orders had been sent to submarine commanders to desist from the sinking of passenger ships. On the basis of these various declarations Wilson felt justified in transmitting the correspondence to the Allies. He had brought the Germans a long way; they were now in no position to reverse the process of concession; it was clear that the armistice would be what the Allied commanders decided that it ought to be.

This point has been frequently missed by the critics of Woodrow Wilson. He has been charged with softness towards Germany. The charge is not substantiated by the facts. At all times he reserved to the Allied military leaders the determination of the military terms which should conclude the war. On the German side, on the other hand, it has been claimed that the President deceived and duped the authorities of the Reich. There is not the slightest evidence to support this claim, either. The Germans yielded because they had to yield; they accepted the Fourteen Points without question—they did not dare debate them. Indeed, when Prince Max prepared a speech reserving German rights under the Points, the military leaders would not permit him to deliver it. It might, they declared, "endanger the whole armistice action."

It is interesting to observe that the advocates of the stiffest terms were the American military leaders. General Pershing was by no means certain that there ought to be an armistice at all; General Bliss, who participated in the discussions of the Supreme War Council, believed that Germany should be totally disarmed. But Marshal Foch, whose voice was naturally the most influential on the military side, wished only to make it impossible for the Germans to renew the war, and this involved, in his judgment, the surrender of one third of the German artillery and half the machine guns, together with vast quantities of rolling stock, and—most important of all—the right to occupy the principal bridgeheads on the Rhine. On the naval side, the British view was bound to be as weighty as that of Foch on land; the British were satisfied with the surrender of German submarines, and the interning of the battle cruisers and the High Seas Fleet which had been built up at so much pains in the years 1898–1914.

A later generation has been somewhat critical of the conditions imposed on Germany in those fateful days of the fall of 1918. It has been stated again and again that they were not sufficiently severe to impress the German people with the completeness of their defeat, and that it would have been a great deal better for the future peace of the world if the triumphant armies of the Allies had found their way to Berlin, and had marched down the Linden to the music of victory as the Germans had done in Paris in 1871, and were to do again in 1940.

There is much to be said for this view. Certainly, it was not long after the end of the struggle before the pleasant illusion began to crop up among the vanquished that they had been deceived, not conquered, and Hitler, the prince of demagogues, played upon this illusion again and again both before his rise to power and after he was firmly installed. It might have been better if the Allies had been more drastic. But however this may be, we must not blame Woodrow Wilson. The terms of the armistice were not fixed by the President of the United States. They were fixed by the military leaders.

In another respect, however, the role of President Wilson was of great importance. It was undoubtedly in large part due to him that the German Emperor abdicated and the German Republic began its troubled history.

In each of his notes to Prince Max of Baden, the President had asked the question, "For whom does the German government speak?" In his final note of October 23, indicating that he would transmit the request for an armistice to the Allies, he declared, "If we must deal with the military masters and the monarchical autocrats . . . it [the government of the United States] must demand, not peace negotiations, but surrender." Whatever may have lain behind these phrases (and the facts are still obscure), they were bound to make the Germans believe that the overthrow of the Emperor was connected with their best hopes for the future; as early as October 25 the Prime Minister of Bavaria and his Minister of War expressed this opinion. During the next fortnight the sentiment grew; it grew not only among the political leaders, but among the soldiers and sailors; and on the eighth of November the Chancellor sent word to the reluctant monarch that it was time that he laid down his crown. On the ninth the Kaiser crossed the Dutch frontier; the government had proclaimed his abdication in advance of his decision. The First German Empire was at an end.

Opinions may well differ as to whether these last political developments were in the interests of European reconstruction. The German Constitution had already been modified to make the Chancellor responsible to the Reichstag, and so to the representatives of the German people. Was this not enough? Would not the monarchy have presented a more successful barrier to the vulgarities and brutalities of National Socialism than the undignified and somewhat futile government set up at Weimar? And did not Wilson bring down the wrong duck? Was it not the German General Staff, not the German Emperor, that constituted the most sinister and dangerous element in the German state? Did not the shift to a republican régime to a certain extent disguise the fact that the German military caste was far from discredited or driven from power? This much at least we may say. Democratic government in Germany began under any but happy auspices; it was perhaps inevitable, but certainly unfortunate, that it was from the beginning identified with defeat and disaster. That it never enjoyed a very high prestige, and was at times subjected to severe humiliation, has something to do with the rise of Adolf Hitler and National Socialism.

The victory won by President Wilson in the overthrow of the Imperial régime in Germany was, in the perspective of a brief space of fifteen years, to prove a barren one. It was, alas! much the same with another, and, as it seemed at the time, a greater success. Before the Germans were called to Compiègne to sign the armistice, the Allied governments had accepted the Fourteen Points, with only minor reservations. This acceptance was due to Colonel House, who represented the President in the momentous sessions of the Supreme Council in October and November, 1918. There were some heated moments before the Colonel had his way; he was obliged at one point to hint at the possibility of a separate peace on the part of the United States; and there was a very difficult obstacle to be got over in British resistance to the American doctrine of the freedom of the seas. To this point Wilson attached a very great importance. But the matter was finally settled by an agreement on the part of the British to discuss the matter at the Peace Conference; and the only other qualification of the Points that was accepted by the American representative was a definition of reparations (reparations themselves having been agreed upon as consistent with the Wilsonian tenets) as "damages done to civilians and their property on land, on sea, and in the air." The Germans were duly notified of these two reservations, and the actual signing of the armistice was based upon the principles that had been enunciated by the President, with the modifications just mentioned.

It is necessary to say here, however, that as a blueprint for the making of peace the Fourteen Points were to exhibit numerous defects. Some of the questions which were most to trouble the postwar world, for example the question of German Austria, of the Sudetenland, of Shantung, were not covered by them at all. Some questions which they *did* cover — the freedom of the seas, the lowering of economic barriers — were not even discussed by the Peace Conference. On the matter of reparations, destined to be one of the most troubling problems of the first postwar decade, the President's language, even when supplemented by the gloss of the pre-armistice agreement, was not sufficiently exact to prevent a host of difficulties from arising. On many of the various boundary questions that came before the Conference, Wilson's phraseology, though not always wholly precise, did indeed establish a point of reference, a basis of decision; but it did not prevent the French or the Italians from bringing forward and contending for proposals entirely incompatible with his ideals, nor did the final settlements correspond in all instances with the strictest interpretation of his principles. The President, indeed, would have been free to fight, and would, it may be assumed, have fought in actuality for many of the things for which he strove in Paris if the Fourteen Points had never been accepted by the Allies; and it is at least questionable how much strength he was ever to draw in any specific controversy from the agreement to which those same Allies had put their names. Nor were the Points more satisfactory in their relation to German opinion. To the peace which resulted at Versailles the Germans were never reconciled, as a peace of idealism and justice; and it is less important to ascertain whether they were justified or not in their complaints and lamentations than it is to note that, in practice, the Wilsonian platform provided no basis for the reconciliation of the moral outlook of the victors and the vanquished.

## Summary

*How should one sum up the Wilsonian diplomacy of 1917–1918? To the first of the President's objectives, the ideal of a League of Nations, the Allies and the vanquished had been committed; the second of these objectives, the attainment of security through the defeat of Germany, had been temporarily accomplished, for the Reich was indeed prostrate; the third objective, the overthrow of the German government which had begun the war, had been achieved; the bases of the peace had been laid in the acceptance of the Fourteen Points. The victory looked like a reasonably complete one.*

*On the other hand, in several respects the war diplomacy of Wilson, in the perspective of 1944, appears to have been less than wise. In the first place, too much faith was placed in a change of Germany's political forms as a guarantee of peace. To imagine that a democratic order in Germany would alter the whole temper of the German nation, to assume that a Republican Germany would be pacific, that a change of form would alter or abolish the profound hold which the militarist and the* Junker *exercised over a docile and politically inept people, was to imagine a vain thing. In the second place, it might have been wiser to bring home more forcefully to the vanquished the fact that they had been defeated. The failure to do this made it possible for the unscrupulous politicians of National Socialism to bring forward the proposition that the Reich had been duped into surrender, and made easier the work of rousing German resentment against the peace of Versailles. In the third place, by his speeches Wilson had encouraged the idea that it was possible to rearrange the map of Europe on the basis of something universally accepted as justice. The idea was an illusion. But of this we shall have more to say in the next chapter.*

# IV

# The Treaty of Versailles

*At Versailles Wilson attempted to erect a new world order, based on a League of Nations. But the League had no adequate force behind it; and the territorial settlements that were made could only be maintained if Germany were kept weak. The economic questions, such as reparations, were not well handled. The exclusion of Russia from the new organization was a fatal defect. Japanese imperialism was given concessions in the Orient. There were some forward steps taken, but they did not balance the deficiencies of the treaty.*

## The Treaty and the League

In undertaking to analyze the Treaty of Versailles, we should relate it to the ideals and objectives which President Wilson had proclaimed during the war. Of these by far the greatest is the ideal of a permanent and lasting peace, an ideal which many Americans have always longed to see realized in fact. The President had led the United States into a general European war reluctantly and only after the exercise of extreme patience, and he had become convinced that a new struggle of the same kind, if it broke out in the future, would inevitably bring the United States within its orbit. In order to prevent such a catastrophe, only one course was open — the participation of the American people and their government in an effective organization for the maintenance of peace.

"I can predict with absolute certainty," he declared in one

of his speeches, "that within another generation there will be another world war if the nations of the world do not concert the method by which to prevent it"; and again, "Unless we concert measures to prevent it . . . the next time will come; it will come while this generation is living, and the children will be sacrificed upon the altar of that war." How prophetic these words seem today; with what deep sincerity the President analyzed the problem that he had set out to solve.

It was this sincerity, of course, that had much to do with the President's decision to attend the Peace Conference in person; from first to last, from the armistice to his final retirement from office, one might say, he burned with zeal for the realization of this great ideal. He believed that the organization of a League of Nations was not only a necessary, but the first and the most fundamental, business of the men who met at Paris in the winter of 1919; by force of will and deep conviction he succeeded as early as January 25, only eight days after the opening of the conference, in having the question of the League made the business of a special commission over which he presided; he drove this commission forward in many an evening meeting with ruthless energy, and secured the completion of the first draft of the so-called Covenant by the time he was compelled to return to America on February 14, 1919. The general outline of the Covenant was defined within a month after the plenipotentiaries gathered at Paris. Tenacious and farsighted as the President was, however, he fell far short of success in realizing his ideal.

## The Weakness of the League

The central idea of the League, in theory, was the idea of common action against an aggressor state. It was to be a League to *enforce* peace; it was, in Wilson's view, to substitute for a system of alliance, a concert of power on the part of all the states of the world against aggression. The state which went to war was to be punished; and it was to know that it would be punished before it went to war. Looking at the matter from this point of view, the Covenant of the League of Nations is, I think it must be conceded, very far from satisfactory; it fails to carry out in fact what was agreed upon in theory. In the first place, there is in it no complete prohibition on warlike action. There are cases under the Covenant where war is permitted. But there is something still more important. The Covenant provided machinery that was wholly inadequate for the discipline of a state which went to war contrary to its provisions. It did not genuinely provide for effective common coercive action against an aggressor. In Article 16 it stipulated for the application of certain sanctions against a lawbreaking state. This article is very clear as to the rupture of economic relations with such a state, very clear and very specific. But observe its weasel words when it comes to the use of force. "It shall be the duty of the Council in such case to recommend to the several Governments concerned what effective military, naval or air force the Members of the League shall severally contribute to the armed forces to be used to protect the covenants of the League." Not a word of any binding obligation; not a hint of a definite pledge to use force against the disturber of the peace. And it is the same way with regard to Article 10, by which the League members agree to "respect and preserve as against external aggression the territorial integrity and existing political independence of all members of the League." All that is stated is, "The Council shall advise as to the means by which this obligation shall be fulfilled."

In other words, when it came to the forthright avowal of

the necessity for putting force behind the obligations of the Covenant, and stating this fact in perfectly clear and unequivocal language, the issue was evaded.

Those who saw this point most clearly were undoubtedly the French. On more than one occasion in the course of the discussion they expressed their desire for an international force which should be able to carry out the prescriptions of the Covenant. There may have been good reasons why the President could not accept such a view. American opinion was by no means prepared for such a great departure from precedent; and it was possible, also, to raise certain constitutional objections to putting American soldiers under external control. But the point does not lie in Wilson's refusal to accept the French scheme; it lies in the failure to meet the issue of force at all. Whether an international organization for the maintenance of peace is feasible or impracticable is not for any one individual to say; but that such an organization must rest on force, and must in some form have force behind it, seems to be demonstrated by the teaching of experience.

It is not difficult to understand why the issue was not faced at Paris in 1919. For the United States and for Great Britain also, the idea of a world alliance to keep the peace (and nothing less than this was involved in the League theory) was a long step away from traditional policy; and, more than this, the English-speaking peoples, again and again in their history, have shown by the trend of their public opinion, and by the policies of their statesmen, a genuine reluctance to face such a harsh truth. Accustomed to the processes of compromise and adjustment in their internal political life, ruled (to their honor be it said) by the processes of public opinion rather than by arbitrary power, they instinctively shrink in international affairs from the invocation of the sword. Pacifist they are not and never have been; but reluctant to fight unless

forced to do so they showed themselves in 1914 and 1917 and again in 1938 and 1941.

Because it owed much to British and American draftsmen, then, the Covenant scamped the central issue that was involved in a League to Enforce Peace; it relied rather on economic pressure than on physical force. We can see today that this was wrong, and has been proved wrong by time. For in 1935 the League machinery was invoked, or at any rate partially invoked, against the Italian conquest of Ethiopia; and it was discovered that in order to apply the economic boycott the nations concerned had to be ready to fight if the boycott were regarded as just cause of war. Because the British government, the spearhead of the movement for the coercion of Italy, did not really have the courage of its convictions, because it was not really ready to face the ultimate consequences of its action, the movement failed; and if it failed against Italy, economically by no means a strong state, how much more likely that it would fail against a truly powerful nation. At any rate, there is nothing in the experience of the last twenty years that justifies the belief that economic pressure is a substitute for war or a dependable instrument for keeping the peace. In putting economic pressure in the forefront and force in the background, the framers of the Covenant committed a fundamental error. We may say, if we like, that the world was not ready for more drastic doctrine, and excuse their action on this ground; but we will not by such excuses have altered in any degree the facts of the case, or the necessity (if we are to build upon the past) of recognizing the error.

In his first and fundamental objective, then, the creation of a really strong League to *enforce* peace, the President failed from the beginning. From the first, moreover, the most harshly realistic of the statesmen at Paris knew that he had failed. The demonstration of this fact lies complete before our eyes in one important episode. When it came to the question of the Rhineland, the French adopted a very stiff position indeed with regard to its long-term garrisoning; and in order to bring them to a more reasonable frame of mind, it was necessary for the President to give his consent to nothing less than a treaty of alliance, with Great Britain and France, by which the two English-speaking peoples were to come to the aid of their continental ally in case she were attacked by Germany. That Clemenceau, the venerable Prime Minister of France, should demand this compact was consistent enough with the quality of his mind, and with his memories of German violence; that it was accepted by Lloyd George and President Wilson amounted to a confession that the machinery of the Covenant could not be depended upon in and of itself to prevent war. It may be that neither of these statesmen realized the full implications of his action; but those implications were nonetheless there and nonetheless fundamental. The security of France and of Europe depended upon the armed power of the democracies. That the Covenant did not take full account of this fact, that it had to be supplemented by an alliance, was an implied confession of its weakness and inadequacy.

## Reduction of Armaments

The same lack of realism, it may appear to us today, that is to be found in the drafting of the Covenant appears also in the discussions at Paris with regard to the disarmament of Germany. That there should be a sharp reduction of German armament was, of course, on all sides taken for granted. But neither the President nor Mr. Lloyd George was ready to carry the principle of reduction of German armament to its logical conclusion. Neither of them was ready to provide in the treaty for that systematic inspection of German military establishment that was indispensable if the terms of the treaty were to mean anything in practice. Neither seems to have been in the least concerned that the German General Staff was left intact, to nurse its wounds and prepare for its own vindication. The insistence of the French on "inspection" was brushed aside. It was stated in the treaty that German disarmament was to furnish a basis for a general reduction of armaments. This was sound Wilsonian principle. But no adequate provision was made to see to it that the effectiveness of German disarmament was guaranteed by appropriate machinery. That in such circumstances France should be left suspicious and reluctant to reduce her own military establishment appears less remarkable today than it did in 1919.

## Territorial Settlements

If the Covenant of the League and the arms provisions of the treaty were unsatisfactory as a basis of organized peace, what is to be said of the territorial terms of the treaty? In judging these, we have to take into account the principle upon which they were based, the principle of self-determination, the principle that in the fixing of new boundaries the wishes of the populations concerned should be the dominating consideration.

It is easy to see why this conception bulked large in the minds of the peacemakers of 1919. Europe in 1914 was full of *irredenta,* of regions whose populations desired to live under some other government than that which actually governed them. The intensity of these feelings had only grown with the war itself. The ambition of the Poles, of the Czechoslovaks, of the Rumanians, of the Serbs, to reconstitute truly national states according to their dreams was matched by the French desire to recover Alsace-Lorraine, or by the yearnings of the Irish for freedom. To ignore these ambitions was a practical impossibility; and to satisfy them, now that German military power was dissolved, seemed not only the wisest, but in many ways the easiest course. Furthermore, the whole idea of national self-determination was closely connected with the democratic ideal; it was based on a principle dear to the heart of Americans, and deeply cherished by the President himself; it seemed to be the vindication of the fundamental conceptions of American polity. To have denied the liberated peoples of Europe their just rights would have seemed nothing less than a monstrosity; such a thought could hardly be considered in the climate of opinion of 1919.

But it by no means follows that the principle of self-determination was a conclusive method of handling territorial questions. The various European nationalities are so intermingled, especially in Eastern Europe, that it is impossible to draw any frontier which will not leave some national minorities under the rule of other national majorities. Such situations had often caused heartburnings in the past, and were bound to do so again. No settlement that could be devised could or would make everybody happy.

And there is more to the matter than this. It is easy to talk about the wishes of a given population, but difficult to find out what those wishes are. They might be different at one time than at another. They might be different in good times than in bad. They might be different under the impulse of a vigorous propaganda than in a quiet situation. There is no final answer to the vexing questions of boundary in the application of the idea of national choice. It may well be, indeed, that a different technique will be applied in the years after the present war. Perhaps as satisfactory an international arrangement as any of the years after Versailles was the Greco-Turkish agreement of 1921. In this case peace and concord were arrived at by an exchange of populations, not by merely fixing a frontier. It might have been better if this idea had been applied in other instances. At any rate, in drawing the various boundaries at Paris the peacemakers inevitably left a good many problems unsolved.

It cannot be said, however, that President Wilson, in his role of peacemaker, paid no heed to what might be considered as the just rights of the defeated nation. On the western frontier of Germany, for example, in concert with Mr. Lloyd George, he strenuously and successfully opposed that section of French opinion which sought to detach the Rhineland from the Reich. A small area, the Saar, was put under international government for fifteen years on the hypothesis that only so could France utilize fully the coal of this region, coal which she needed to make up for the devastation of her northern mines. But at the end of this period, a plebiscite under carefully defined conditions was to take place, and the overwhelming vote by which in 1935 the people declared in favor of return to Germany ended all discussion of the question. Alsace-Lorraine, of course, went back to France, but it is probable, if not certain, that this was the desire of its inhabitants in 1919. The Polish frontier also was drawn with due regard for the principle of self-determination. It was Mr. Lloyd George rather than Mr. Wilson, it is true, who insisted that Danzig, an almost wholly German city, should not go to Poland, and who took the lead in demanding plebiscites along much of the new German-Polish frontier. But in the decisive moments the President sided with the British Premier, rather than with the French, and he deserves some credit for the result. It is a flat misrepresentation of the facts to describe the Polish boundary of 1919 as grossly unjust to Germany, if the principle of nationality be taken as the criterion.

There were other instances where one cannot be so complacent. The treaty provided that German Austria, which had become an independent republic after the breakup of the Dual Monarchy, could be united with Germany only after the consent of the Council of the League of Nations. This, in effect, meant that either France or Italy could veto such a union. Whatever we may think of the probability that a vote in 1919 would have resulted in the annexation of Austria to the Reich, we must concede that the provision just cited was a denial of the idea of self-determination where its application would favor Germany. The President seems to have made no serious effort to have it otherwise. In the second place, the inclusion of the so-called Sudetenland, the provinces which came to Hitler in 1938, in the new republic of Czechoslovakia, whether justified on other grounds or not, was a violation of Wilsonian theory. Here again there are no indications that Wilson had anything to say on the matter. But while the idea of nationality furnished a basis for many of the territorial decisions, in the two cases where that theory ran in favor of the Reich it was entirely ignored. At a later date the practical effect of this action was to furnish a plausible rallying cry to the forces of discontent in Germany, and to weaken the belief in the justice of the settlement in the victor nations as well. So much is clearly established.

But if we concentrate all our attention on the justice or injustice of the territorial arrangements of Versailles (assuming that either of these words has an exact and precise meaning) we shall miss a point that is more important. These arrangements could last only if Germany were kept weak. They certainly would not stand against a revived German militarism. Nor was there any reason to assume that if the Reich again became strong, it would rectify the "unjust" settlements and let the "just" settlements stand. The question was one not of right, but of power. So it was to be demonstrated, when Adolf Hitler came to power. For the Fuehrer, in 1938 and 1939, was by no means willing to stop with the annexation of Austria and the absorption of the Sudetenland (acts which found their defenders in the democratic nations), but went on to the suppression of the liberties of the Czechs, and the attack on Poland. As one contemplates these facts, written large in the record of our time, it is clear that the error of Versailles lay in the fact that the settlements made there were not supported by sufficient power. Just as the League needed force behind it, the new map of Europe needed force behind it. Had the force existed, the map might not have been challenged. Or if it had been changed at all, it would have been by less violent processes.

## Russia and the Versailles Settlement

There is a final aspect of the European settlements of 1919 that must challenge our attention before we attempt to summarize the conclusions of this chapter. They were made without the participation of the greatest of European nations; they were made without consulting or entering into any direct negotiations with Russia. They left the greatest of all European states outside the new international system, isolated and in a sense outlawed. An understanding of the policy of the Allies towards Russia during the Peace Conference is essential if we are to appreciate correctly the period which followed, or draw the appropriate comparisons and contrasts between 1919 and the epoch of today.

In his attitude towards Russia Wilson undeniably began with the most idealistic purposes. The sixth of the Fourteen Points declared for the evacuation of all Russian territory, and such a settlement of all questions affecting Russia as would provide her with "an unhampered opportunity for the independent determination of her own political development and national policy and assure her of a sincere welcome into the society of free nations under institutions of her own choosing. . . . The treatment accorded Russia," the President went on, "will be the acid test of their good will, of their comprehension of her needs as distinguished from their interests, and of their intelligent and unselfish sympathy."

To translate these words into deeds, however, was a matter of the utmost difficulty. The government set up by the Bolshevik revolution was bound to arouse intense antagonism in many circles of the Western World, an antagonism redoubled in intensity by the peace of Brest-Litovsk, which left the Allied states to pursue the struggle against Germany alone. Before the war was over, the United States had felt the impact of this antagonism, and had seen its own policy affected by the attitude of its associates in the war. In European Russia, the violent hostility of many Britons and Frenchmen to the Bolshevik régime resulted in an intervention in the Archangel district, in which American troops participated, and helped to sustain there an anti-Bolshevik régime. In Siberia, a variety of circumstances brought about similar action. For reasons that are still obscure, French and British policy, as early as the end of 1917, appears to have encouraged the occupation of Vladivostok and Eastern Siberia by the Japanese. The idea was formally broached to the American State Department in January of the next year. It was by no means received with enthusiasm. As time went on, and the pressure increased, the American government began to weaken. The revolt of the Czechoslovak prisoners in Siberia against the Soviet régime, the argument that these heroic fighters needed assistance, the humanitarian appeal to restore some kind of order in a disorganized region, and the conviction that if the United States did not act the Japanese might act alone, finally induced President Wilson to authorize the sending of troops to this remote part of the world. The statement in which he announced his intention was carefully guarded. The sole duty of the expeditionary force, he declared, was to assist the Czechs, help steady Russian efforts at self-government, and guard Allied military stores. The American occupation of Siberia, in the main, pursued the objectives thus defined. But it was not likely that the Bolshevik régime at Moscow would regard such operations with enthusiasm, and it was certain that, indirectly if not directly, the United States would become involved in the anti-Bolshevik maneuvers of its European associates.

By the time the Peace Conference convened at Paris, the climate of opinion, both in America and in Europe, was wholly unfavorable to an understanding with the leaders of the Russian Revolution, and the admission of Russia to a place in the state system that was to be reconstituted at Paris. There were strong elements in both France and Great Britain which believed that the only wise policy was the support of the anti-Bolshevik factions; the most eminent exponent of this point of view was the British Secretary of State for War, whose name was Winston Churchill; and the practicability of such a policy seemed in part to be borne out by the presence of governments hostile to the Soviet in the Ukraine under General Denikin and at Omsk in Siberia under Admiral Kolchak. To this ill-fated policy (and ill-fated and disastrous it certainly proved to be) President Wilson never gave any substantial support; but he was utterly unable to forge an alternative. He earnestly supported Mr. Lloyd George in the early days of the conference in seeking to bring about a meeting of the various Russian factions on the island of Prinkipo in the Sea of Marmora. The project died a-borning, and though it was the anti-Bolshevik régimes which rejected it most flatly, it is difficult to believe that it would have been possible to reconcile the ambitions, ideals and practical purposes of Lenin and Trotsky with those of the Russian Whites. The famous Bullitt mission to Moscow, undertaken with an eye to direct negotiation with the Soviets, would in any case have aroused the bitterest opposition, but the military successes of the Omsk government in April and May made certain its failure. At the end of the latter month the President joined the leaders of the other great states in assurances to Admiral Kolchak that he would be assisted with munitions, supplies and food, if he would give satisfactory guarantees as to the democratic character of his régime, and consent to the calling of a constituent assembly. While actual recognition was never extended, and while the collapse of the régime settled the question in November, American policy was now moving in the direction of clearer and clearer hostility to the government in Moscow. In the proscription of the Bolsheviks, as time went on, and long before Wilson retired from office, the United States was not to lag behind the nations of Western Europe. While American troops were withdrawn from Archangel as early as the spring of 1919, and from Siberia in the winter of 1920, while at no time did the American government commit itself so deeply to positive assistance to the enemies of the Bolsheviks as did the French and the British, it made no bones of its repugnance to the Bolshevik régime, its distrust of its good faith, its dislike of its authoritarian character, its feeling that there would not be "any common ground upon which it could stand with a power whose conceptions of international relations are so entirely alien to its own, so utterly repugnant to its moral sense." When Woodrow Wilson left office in 1921, the ostracism of the Russian government by the victor powers of 1918 was complete. The welcome for Russia in the "society of free nations" which Wilson envisaged in the Fourteen Points was to be indefinitely postponed.

## Economic Terms of the Treaty

It was neither the territorial terms of the Treaty of Versailles nor the exclusion of Russia from the councils of Europe that produced the greatest friction in the decade following the peace settlement. The irritations of 1919–1929 centered about the question of reparations. The decisions taken at Paris undeniably shaped for the worse the history of the next decade. It is, therefore, necessary for us to see what those decisions were, to indicate how they came to be, and how, with regard to them, President Wilson sustained one of his most serious defeats.

From the summer of 1917, in his reply to the peace overture of the Pope, Wilson had clearly expressed his opposition to "punitive damages" of any kind. His view of the matter had prevailed in the drafting of the armistice agreement, which declared that Germany must pay reparations for damages done to civilians and their property "on land, on sea and in the air." The first efforts to go beyond this declaration met with his vigorous opposition. He took a firm and, as it proved, a successful stand against the effort of the French Finance Minister and the Australian Premier at Paris to assess against Germany the whole cost of the war. His victory was only temporary, and it was one of form rather than substance. For, having been beaten when they attacked directly, the advocates of great indemnities made a successful flanking movement. They brought forward the propositions that pensions fell within the definition of reparations incorporated in the armistice. It was sophistry, and nothing else, which made it possible to argue that pensions were "damages" done to civilians. When first approached on this matter, the President seems to have rejected any such idea. But beset by General Jan Smuts, in whom he had much confidence, whose liberalism was as sincere and well-known as that of Wilson himself, the President yielded. From the angle of intellectual honesty, no decision that he made at Paris is more reprehensible.

In the discussions on this important subject of reparations, the President's advisers and the President himself strove for two clear objectives: to limit the reparations payments to a fixed amount, and to limit the payment of that amount in time. On both these questions they were defeated. In its final form, it is true, the treaty did call upon the Reparations Commission, the body charged with the calculation of the obligations of the Reich, to fix Germany's total burden by the first of May, 1921; and it also directed the Commission to draw up a schedule of payments for the discharge of the entire obligation within a period of thirty years. But the sum which might be arrived at under the schedules of "damages" set up in the treaty was certain to be an astronomical one; and the article which specified for a schedule of payments for a period of thirty years made it clear that Germany's obligations might be extended beyond that time.

Of course it can be argued that in the existing state of public opinion, the only practicable manner of dealing with the whole question, was to postpone the decision to a future when reason might be more certain to prevail; and this defense has been and will be offered for the American negotiators at Paris. Indeed it may have substantial validity. But it cannot alter the fact that with regard to reparations the treaty was not what Wilson, or his advisers, would have had it; and that nowhere was the American point of view more completely thrust into the background than in dealing with this particular question.

It is in connection with this reparations question, also, that appears the famous war-guilt clause of the Treaty of Versailles.

In order to satisfy the strident public opinion of Britain and France, Lloyd George and Clemenceau insisted upon proclaiming in theory what they were not able to get accepted in practice, that is, the responsibility of Germany for the total costs of the war. The result was the famous Article 231, which spoke of "all the loss and damage to which the Allied and Associated Governments and their nations have been subjected as a consequence of the war imposed upon them by the aggression of Germany and her allies."

That Woodrow Wilson had anything much to do with this declaration does not at all appear. But no one can deny that, even if we assume it to be true, it was wholly unwise. It was naturally not accepted by most Germans as expressing the actual facts, and it furnished a ready argument to Hitlerian demagogy. It unnecessarily irritated and affronted German opinion, and contributed to the German feeling that the entire treaty was unfair and unjust.

## The Pacific Colonies of Germany and Shantung

If the Treaty of Versailles was by no means beyond criticism as regards Germany, so it must be regarded as paving the way for the advance of a militarist Japan. The Japanese had entered the war in 1914. They had naturally picked up a fair share of the islands that had belonged to Germany. The British and the French had by treaty recognized their right to keep their plunder. President Wilson found himself confronted by a difficult situation. To compel Japan to give up her gains was impossible. The President hoped, however, to impose some slight check upon her through the application of a new principle to the colonies of the Reich. These colonies were not to be ceded outright, but were to be organized as mandates, under international supervision. The degree of authority exercised by the so-called mandatory power was to vary in different cases, but in all instances was carefully defined in Article 22 of the Covenant. With regard to the islands of the Pacific, Japan was given almost complete control, but she was bound by a solemn pledge not to fortify them. This pledge she was, of course, to violate in due time, and to install herself in the Marshalls and the Carolines so securely as to cost the United States a great national effort to drive her out.

More important than the colonial question, at any rate in the opinion of contemporaries, was the question of Shantung. The policy of the United States with regard to China from 1900 to 1939 may almost be compressed into a single sentence. For a variety of reasons, partly commercial, partly sentimental and moral, the people and the government of the United States have consistently sympathized with China, and frowned upon projects to despoil her. At the same time, they have never, up to the present moment, been in a position to prevent what they have unequivocally condemned. In no other department of American diplomacy has the gulf between high principles and effective performance been wider. For not only was American opinion never ready, until Pearl Harbor, to use the ultimate weapon of force in the Orient, but the United States has never had any really wholehearted support for its own position from any other power. On the concrete question of Shantung, the American position at Paris could hardly have been worse. The German leasehold at Kiaochow had been occupied by Japan at the cost of blood and treasure. The Chinese government had agreed to extensive Japanese privileges in the province by the agreement of May 25, 1915, and again by an agreement of September 24, 1918, and the second agreement had been accompanied by a large advance payment on a railway loan; the Japanese had secured the assent of their allies to the transfer of German rights in China at the end of the war; the United States itself, in one of the most controverted documents in our diplomatic history (the Lansing-Ishii memorandum), had recognized that Japan had "special interests" in China. All these considerations taken together put President Wilson in a most unfortunate situation when it came to the discussion of Shantung at the Peace Conference. Nor was this all. In the presentation of their demands the Japanese delegation at Paris showed great adroitness and the most accurate possible timing. On April 11, the President in the discussions of the League Commission had been obliged to rule that the so-called racial-equality amendment to the Covenant, an amendment earnestly desired by the Japanese, though phrased in the most innocent and ineffective terms, had been rejected. Within the next fortnight he had had his famous quarrel with the Italian delegation, which resulted in the departure of the latter from Versailles, and the fear that they might not come back for the signing of the treaty. It was under these circumstances that the Japanese brought forward their demand for the recognition of their claims with regard to Shantung.

In such circumstances, the President was bound to suffer a defeat. He was compelled to assent to three articles in the treaty which provided for the transfer of German rights to Japan. He was not able to incorporate in these articles any mention of the repeated pledge of Japan to restore Chinese sovereignty in the peninsula. He was able only to secure a declaration from Japan stating it to be Japanese policy to hand back the province to China, "retaining only the economic privileges granted to Germany, and the right to establish a settlement under the usual conditions at Tsing-tao." This declaration was qualified by clauses which asserted Japanese intention to retain special police on the railway line, and it was made public by the Japanese only after substantial pressure on the part of the United States, and only some weeks after the signature of the peace treaty. It provided a basis for further negotiation, a point of departure for the American government, but can hardly be said to have done more. Wilsonian idealism, as the President himself realized with intense bitterness, sustained a severe defeat when applied to the questions of the Orient.

It is interesting to observe the terms in which Wilson sought to allay his own pangs of regret at the concessions he was forced to make. His hope, as he told Ray Stannard Baker, lay in the League, which would redeem the errors of the past, and make all things whole. It lay in the League, not as an instrument of coercion, but as an instrument of moral pressure. It is easy to understand this. It is of the very essence of the democratic spirit — this faith in the power of opinion. But the faith is a delusive one. In the world of international politics as it exists today, as this generation has learned by harsh experience, the ultimate arbiter, yes, the ultimate arbiter of moral principle, is force. In refusing to face this fact squarely, Wilson was only a typical American; yet the refusal to face it has much to do with some of the difficulties into which our foreign policy has fallen.

## Other Aspects of the Treaty and Wilson's Leadership

From what has so far been set down, it would appear that the judgment on the Treaty of Versailles, and on Woodrow Wilson as one of its sponsors, must be very unfavorable. There is another side to the picture, one that ought not to be ignored. Take, for example, the question of the League. It may be true that the League was not adequate to the great task designed for it. But it was not without its uses. The mandatory provisions, for example, though in many respects defective, were at least an attempt to establish the principle of international control of backward territories and of peoples not yet ready for self-government. This principle enjoys much popularity today, and we may see it revived at the end of the present war. The League itself proved to be useful in many respects: as a center of international administration in a wide variety of nonpolitical matters; as a clearinghouse for the collection of much useful information; as a means of bringing together without fuss and feathers statesmen from all over the world and permitting them to discuss their problems in a calm and neutral atmosphere. The territorial settlements reached in Paris, whatever their defects, were in many instances an honest attempt to deal with very difficult problems. They certainly reduced in very large measure the number of Europeans living under a hateful alien rule. Some of their "injustices" do not seem so shocking today as they did then. Even the denial of the right of Austria to unite with Germany, or the putting of the Sudeten Germans under Czech rule, wears a different look when we see the use that an expanded Germany has made of its power. Whatever the irritations created by the reparations clauses, and however unworkable they proved in practice, it is not difficult to understand why an effort was made to extract from the Reich some compensation for the ruin of Belgium and the devastation of France. The men at Paris worked, as statesmen always work, within the limits of existing public opinion. They must be judged with this fact always in mind.

It is not difficult, moreover, to make a charitable or even a friendly judgment with regard to Woodrow Wilson. It is easy to say that the President failed to carry out at Paris the ideals which he had proclaimed during the war. Of course he did. No practical statesman has ever realized his ideals, and none is likely to. Men always fall short of the full realization of their desires. Wilson's error lay in leading the world to expect so much so soon, in his too easy assumption that a new order would be born in Paris, purged of all the vices of the old. He spoke in unhappily apocalyptic terms. To a certain extent his fame has been the victim of the extravagant hopes that he aroused.

In his conviction that a new war would ensue if the victor nations did not concert measures to prevent it, Wilson has never appeared more nearly right than he does in the perspective of 1944. In the more concrete questions of the peace, if we judge him by his motives, by the direction of his thinking, by the courage and disinterestedness which he brought to the solution of his problems, he appears as a great man. He certainly does not suffer by comparison with any of his colleagues.

### The Essence of the Matter

*The fundamental weakness of the Treaty of Versailles, moreover, was one that he could not have cured. That weakness, it cannot be too often repeated, lay in the absence of an effective organized force for the preservation of the peace that had been established. In failing to establish such a force, Wilson merely reflected the views of those whom he represented. In 1919 and 1920, to put the matter bluntly and clearly, the American people were not ready to co-operate with other nations to uphold the peace of the world by a concert of power. They must be more ready, much more ready, at the end of the present war. Only if they are ready and resolute will it be possible in the years ahead to establish an international order in which men can dwell in peace, and rebuild their social and economic institutions in an atmosphere of confidence and hope.*

# V

## The Intermediate Years

*In the years between 1914 and 1939 the alliance that had beaten Germany disintegrated. The United States showed a constant reluctance to use physical force as an instrument of policy, thus reducing its influence in Europe. The Neutrality Acts had the same effect. In the Orient, the American government virtually abdicated, so far as the politics of power were concerned. At the end of the period there was a reaction, however, and by 1939 the same prejudices as to Britain and Germany prevailed as in 1914, and were much intensified. Japan, also, was an object of dislike. It was becoming clear that the American people would not stand aside from world affairs any more than they had a quarter of a century before.*

### Disintegration of the Grand Alliance

Within twenty-one years of the armistice of November 11, 1918, German armies were once again upon the march in a war of aggression more obvious and more perilous than that of 1914. Why was this the case? The answer does not lie solely in the policy of the United States. It lies, in part, in the disintegration of the alliance that had brought Germany to terms. It lies in the failure on the part of the great European powers to maintain the concert of action that had won the war. We need to understand that part of the story in order to put American diplomacy in its proper perspective. Let us then briefly review it.

Of the powers which contended against Germany in the First World War one of the greatest, Russia, as we have already seen, had withdrawn in 1917. From the moment of the Bolshevik revolution until at least the end of the twenties the Russian government stood, for the most, apart from the rest of Europe, isolated, mistrusted, and jealous of the apparent success of European reconstruction. As a factor in the maintenance of the new order created by Versailles, it was negligible; as a constructive force it can hardly be said to have counted at all.

The second rift in the Grand Alliance was opened when Italy was denied the realization of her full ambitions at Paris. President Wilson, in obedience to his principles, could hardly have consented to the execution of the Treaty of London, by which the Dalmatian coast was to come under Italian dominion; he found himself equally unready to recognize the Italian claims to the port of Fiume, which did not come within the scope of that treaty. Nor were France and Great Britain ready at one and the same time to give to the greedy government at Rome everything promised at London and Fiume besides. The climax came when, in a maneuver the failure of which might have been predicted in advance, President Wilson appealed to the Italian people over the heads of the ministry; the Italian representatives at Paris, Orlando and Sonnino, withdrew in high dudgeon; the Italian people gave themselves up to an orgy of patriotism, and gratified their emotions by changing the names of the streets which they had named after Woodrow Wilson in December and January to Via Fiume in April; and the seeds were planted of an Italian discontent that was, whether merely latent or openly expressed, to have much to do with the course of events that followed.

It was not long before Great Britain began to revert to that policy of balance which has often characterized her Continental policy. The course she pursued was never one of the complete abandonment of her French connection, though Anglo-French relations were severely strained when in 1923 the French insisted upon collecting reparations from Germany by the military occupation of the Ruhr; but when it was attempted to supplement the peace treaties by new agreements in 1924 and 1925 Britain made it clear that she would undertake no binding commitments with regard to the eastern frontiers of Germany. None too confident of Britain, French diplomacy constructed the series of alliances known as the Little Entente, by which the Succession States of Versailles, Poland, Czechoslovakia, Rumania, and Yugoslavia were brought together to maintain the settlements of which they were the beneficiaries. For a time this new balance of power on the continent of Europe maintained itself successfully.

Despite the disintegration of the Grand Alliance in 1929 the general situation in Europe appeared very far from discouraging. In the summer of that year a balanced judgment would have been an optimistic judgment. It was the World Depression, and the events which followed on its train, that again tipped the scales towards armaments and war, bringing about a most unhappy change in Germany itself.

Under favorable circumstances the German Republic would have had a difficult task to maintain itself as a democratic state. It lacked prestige from the outset. Many believe that the French invasion of the Ruhr, already alluded to, and the debauching of the German currency which followed, played a large part in the destruction of those middle-class elements on which German democracy depended. The point can be pressed too far, since a substantial recovery took place in the Reich in the years 1924–1929. But there were always elements which did not accept the Weimar Constitution of 1919, and hated the idea of popular rule. The period of economic stress naturally strengthened these forces. The hard-pressed government of Chancellor Bruening in Germany had to wrestle with domestic discontent and mounting unemployment. The prestige of the republic sank steadily; and a policy of concession that might have bolstered its waning prestige was impossible, in view of French opposition. Perhaps no concessions, however generous, would have arrested the trend towards National Socialism, but at any rate the net result was to bring Adolf Hitler into power. The aged President of the German Republic, von Hindenburg, betrayed the constitution he had sworn to protect; and a political adventurer of boundless ambition and equally boundless unscrupulousness entered upon his sinister career as the leader of the Reich.

Looking backwards today, there ought to have been little doubt as to the forces that Hitler represented; they were indeed clearly understood by such experienced observers as Mr. Messersmith, our very able consul in Berlin; but exhausted by the economic distresses of the preceding years, and lulled into security by false promises, the governments of Europe permitted the rebuilding of German armaments and the revival of German power. With a blindness that has its lesson for our present generation, they stood by while the Fuehrer prepared for his career of violence and crime.

It was Britain which had to bear the principal responsibility for these acts of colossal unwisdom. As in the United States, there existed in England much sentiment which regarded the Treaty of Versailles as unjust, and which overlooked the fact that whatever might be the defects of that instrument the revival of German military power under an unscrupulous and ambitious adventurer was a far greater evil and a major peril to world peace. In the early days of Hitlerism there was a tendency in some quarters to regard a strong Reich as a counterpoise to France and a safeguard against Russian Communism. The British moreover, like other peoples, were pre-occupied with the problems of economic recovery; and in the years from 1932 to 1938 British foreign policy was weaker and more futile than at any period in modern history. In vain the French sought a counterweight to British indifference; it was possible, it is true, to bring back into the European picture the great government of Soviet Russia, menaced as was the rest of Europe by German revival; but the new entente between Paris and Moscow was never cordially accepted, either by all elements in France or by France's Continental Allies. The fear of Communism counterbalanced the physical power of the Soviets; and Europe as a whole could by no means make up its mind to risk the one in order to get the benefits of the other. Thus there was no effective opposition to German re-armament; and as that rearmament proceeded, the European balance altered more and more in favor of the Reich. In 1934 the Germans, by a nonaggression pact, began the process of detaching Poland from its French connection, and in this they were aided by Polish fear of Russia; in 1935 discontented Italy embarked upon the Ethiopian adventure, and was thoroughly alienated from France and Great Britain by the ineffectual effort of the League to apply sanctions against her; in 1936 Hitler occupied the demilitarized Rhineland, and succeeded in this most brilliant and most fundamental of all his coups through the indifference and slothfulness of the Baldwin ministry in Great Britain and through excellent diplomatic timing; and from this point on the European situation deteriorated rapidly. The year 1937 saw the beginnings of the Spanish Civil War; the open aid given to the forces of Franco by Italy and Germany was never matched by a resolute policy of support for the Spanish Republic on the part of France and Great Britain; in both countries the conservative elements were lulled into acquiescence by the skillful use of the communist bogey; and the weakness and irresolution of the French and British governments, the profound internal divisions in France, the curious illusion that it was possible to "negotiate" with Hitler, encouraged Fascists and Nazis to raise the price of conciliation again and again. In March of 1938 came the German occupation of Austria; once more the Western powers remained inert; and Hitler marched on to his campaign of violence against Czechoslovakia. It was true that the population of the Sudetenland, of northern Bohemia, was largely German-speaking; it was even true that they had minor grievances against the Czechoslovak state; and capitalizing on these facts the Fuehrer launched a new campaign of agitation, looking to the annexation of this important region. Again he had his way; the French and the British advised the Czechoslovak government to yield to the Reich; even so, war was narrowly avoided; and the conference of Munich represented an immense triumph for the German dictator. It was not only that new lands were acquired; the acquisition of the Sudetenland meant the serious weakening of Czechoslovakia as a barrier to German ambition; while the exclusion of Russia from the Munich Conference profoundly alienated the government at Moscow from the Western powers and paved the way for the Russo-German treaty of friendship of the summer of 1939.

Hitler was quick to seize the advantage he had gained; in March of 1939, in an act of cynical violence which, even for this sinister man, represented the very acme of faithlessness, he occupied Prague and virtually extinguished the Czechoslovak state, and at the same time began a diplomatic campaign against the Poles. But by this time the limits of French and British tolerance had been reached; from London and from Paris came guarantees to the hard-pressed régime at Warsaw; and during the summer of 1939 it was clear to the well-informed that a new German aggression meant war. Nor was the situation changed by the diplomatic coup of August, by which Berlin negotiated a pact of nonaggression with the government at Moscow; the entry of German troops into Poland signalized the beginning of the Second World War. Tardily, and in the worst possible conditions, France and Great Britain finally took up the sword against renascent militarist Germany; at long last the conviction that it was impossible to live at peace with the Nazis had deepened into action. Such, in the briefest possible compass, is the story of 1919 to 1939 from the viewpoint of Europe; and with this résumé in our minds, it is now possible to sketch in more detail the foreign policy of the United States in the corresponding period.

## American Defeat of the League

In the years between 1919 and 1939 the United States contributed both in Europe and in the Orient to the growth of new imperialisms. American policy failed again and again to assess the situation correctly; American action or inaction helped to encourage the forces of disintegration. Let us see in what manner this was so.

The first step in the process was the failure of the United States to ratify the Treaty of Versailles. The defeat of the treaty was the product of a variety of factors, easily understood, but nonetheless deplorable. The President of the United States, for the first time in history, had crossed the Atlantic to take part in a European conference; his voice had been listened to and applauded by European millions. Somehow or other, vaguely rather than concretely, emotionally rather than intellectually, the masses of the Old World had felt new hopes of justice and peace in what he had to say, and in January of 1919 Woodrow Wilson may be said to have occupied a place in the eyes of Western humanity which has rarely been vouchsafed to any individual. Then came the selfishness, the resentments, the jealousies of the Peace Conference. The mood of June was not the mood of January — it was the mood of disillusionment. There was little exaltation and much fear for the future when the peace treaty was signed at Versailles.

That this mood of disillusionment powerfully affected the American people there can be no doubt whatsoever. There were many elements in the United States which were bound to be discontented with the outcome of the Conference. The policy of repression in Ireland pursued by the British after the Easter Rebellion had roused wide resentment in the United States amongst the large Irish-American population, never too enthusiastic about England. The German-Americans were resentful and discontented, and in the nature of the case harsh judges of Wilson's work. The President's quarrel with the Italian delegation affected another important element of our people. But above and beyond these racial groups there were many excellent people who understood little of international politics, and who had responded overcredulously to the Wilsonian vision. Having expected much more than was possible, they were now disposed to judge with excessive harshness what had actually been accomplished. The so-called "liberal" press of 1919 was, in many instances, hostile to the settlement that had been made at Paris.

It is, I think, a fact not to be denied that our political institutions, perhaps it should be said our political habits, give the widest scope to opposition in both foreign and domestic policy. The year and a half before a Presidential election is almost always a period of intense political maneuvering. During this period the party out of power has a professional interest in magnifying all the errors, real or alleged, of those in office, of capitalizing on all their mistakes, of whipping up the maximum hostility, of appealing to every frustrated hope and every unsatisfied sefish desire. There is absolutely nothing in the past history of the United States to suggest that this process stops where foreign affairs are concerned, and that politics ends, "at the water's edge." The precise contrary has been true again and again.

It was natural, then, that the Republican Party should from the beginning conduct a vigorous attack on Woodrow Wilson. Nor was it in the President's temperament to submit to such an attack serenely, or to parry it by a wise and successful strategy. Though his defenders can say with truth that Wilson's appeal for a Democratic Congress in 1918 only paralleled McKinley's appeal for a Republican one in 1898, practically speaking, the appeal was a capital error. Its very lack of success condemned it. From the moment of his departure for Paris, the President was subjected to a political assault which, whether justified or unjustified, in the large owed something to the intensity of his own partisan temper.

I shall not narrate in detail the struggle over the peace treaty in the American Senate. There were certainly members of the opposition who stooped to acts of personal malignity and partisan meanness that it is better to try to forget. There were men who deliberately encouraged the forces of opposition to Wilson at Paris and then turned about and denounced the President for failing to attain his objectives. But we shall never judge the treaty fight correctly unless we understand that much of the opposition was sincere. Partisans are successful only where they have support in the great body of the people. Many sincere men, many good men, seriously doubted the wisdom of American adhesion to the Covenant in the form in which it came back from Paris. They were sometimes moved by traditionalism; they were sometimes moved by an excessive idealism; they were sometimes moved simply by a desire to perfect what they regarded as much less than perfect. All these groups were represented in the opposition to the treaty; all gave strength to the Republicans in their contest with Wilson.

There is one thing still more important to be said. The President could have had his treaty had he been willing to consent to its ratification with reservations. His contention was, of course, that the reservations adopted by the Senate altered the treaty, and that it was impossible, in any case, to negotiate their acceptance with all the signatories who had been present at Versailles. Such a view is entitled to respect. But it would have been far wiser statesmanship to encourage the Senate to accept the compact and then try to secure its acceptance from the other states concerned, than it was to adopt an attitude of bitter opposition. It was a crowning act of folly (to be charitably judged only in view of the President's physical breakdown) to throw the treaty into the confusion, the hurly-burly, the insincerities and equivocations, of a Presidential campaign. In the election of 1920, there was more than the normal amount of political dishonesty; the Republican candidate and the Republican platform were both thoroughly insincere; but many genuine supporters of the League were gulled into supporting Senator Harding, despite the clearest evidence that he neither understood nor cared for the Wilsonian program; they were soon to find that it was not the League supporters, but the irreconcilable foes of the treaty and the Covenant, the "isolationists" as they came to be called, who dominated the situation. The unyielding temper of President Wilson, the reaction against the war and its works, the bitterness of party struggle, the intense feeling of the foes of the treaty, all combined to wreck and ruin the settlement of Paris. By an overwhelming vote Warren Harding was elected President; and one of the first acts of his administration was to make a separate peace with Germany.

*We do not need to overdramatize the importance of this decision. But neither can we minimize it. The abandonment of the Treaty of Versailles was a moral blow to the system that had been set up; the absence of the United States from the League could hardly fail to limit its action, limited enough already; after the defeat of the peace treaty the Anglo-Franco-American treaty of alliance could not even be reported out of committee; the United States had definitely and sharply indicated that it would not back up by effective force the decisions which had been made at Paris. And in the years which followed, efforts to strengthen the machinery of peace were more than once impeded by fear of American resentment, and uncertainty as to what would be the American role if coercive action were taken under the auspices of the League of Nations.*

## Peace by Moral Influence

In place of a diplomacy based upon power, the United States in the twenties and thirties practised a policy based upon moral influence. It was not "isolationist" in the strict sense of the word; but it would make no commitments to assist in the keeping of the peace. It did not stand aloof from the international scene; it did not refuse to participate in international conferences or fail to play a part in important international decisions. The role of its diplomacy was wider than ever before. But that diplomacy was based upon the delusive notion that peace was a matter of good will, of orderly procedure, of verbal promises, rather than a matter of organized power.

The most striking example of this point of view was to be found in the Kellogg Pact of 1928, by which the nations of the world agreed to "renounce" war as "an instrument of national policy." This pact had its origins in a French proposal for a treaty of perpetual friendship between France and the

United States. Under the guidance of the American Secretary of State, Mr. Kellogg, it was widened into a comprehensive agreement by which most of the nations of the world agreed to settle all disputes arising between them by peaceful means. It had behind it an immense body of public opinion; it was widely acclaimed, at least in the United States; it was ratified by the Senate with only a single dissenting vote. By many Americans, sad to say, it was regarded as the perfect solution of the problem of war. It reflected the favorite American illusion, that it is possible to have peace in the world without taking the faintest trouble to maintain it by effective physical force.

Fairness demands that we say of some of the promoters of the pact that they thought of it as opening the way to co-operation with the League. By banning aggressive war, it was hoped, the pact might in due course lead to American participation in positive action against an aggressor state. But the hope proved to be an extravagant one; and it is a sad, but undeniable and obvious fact that the Kellogg treaty proved a feeble barrier to the forces making for war.

Another hope of similar character beguiled the American people in the twenties and the first years of the thirties. Peace, it was believed, might be attained by reduction of armaments. In obedience to this conviction the Harding administration, at the end of 1921, called a conference to meet at Washington to discuss this problem, especially as regarded naval armaments. A treaty was drawn up by which the five great powers, Italy, France, Great Britain, Japan, and the United States, agreed to fixed ratios in capital ships and aircraft carriers, and in the application of these ratios the last three powers mentioned scrapped a not inconsiderable number of vessels actually building. The result was widely hailed as a great triumph for the cause of peace. Eight years later another conference went, in some respects, even further. At London, in the winter of 1930, the United States, Great Britain, and Japan signed a new treaty which limited all types of ships, again according to fixed ratios, and carried the policy of reduction of armaments further than it had ever been carried in modern history.

But there was, very emphatically, another side to the story, and one that was little realized at the time. At Washington, for example, in order to secure the assent of Japan to the 5-5-3 ratio, as it was called, it was necessary for the United States to agree not to fortify the island of Guam, or the Philippines. *To put the matter bluntly, the American government virtually abdicated in the Orient, so far as the use of physical force was concerned.* Perhaps no other course was possible at the time, but the fact remains as stated, and in the perspective of 1944 the concessions then made appear far from wise.

In saying this, we must, of course, be fair. The Harding administration had no intention of abandoning American interests in the Orient, or of reversing the policy of solicitude for China which had so often characterized American policy. It sought to protect the great Chinese Republic by treaty commitments, especially by the so-called Nine-Power Treaty of 1922, which bound its signatories to respect the "administrative integrity" and the "independence" of the state in question. It acted as go-between in an effort to get the Japanese out of Shantung. But it proceeded upon an assumption that was to be proved false with time, the assumption that paper commitments could restrain the onward march of Japanese imperialism.

The fallacy of any such assumption was to be demonstrated in the Manchurian crisis of 1931. In that year the Japanese militarists, in all probability defying their own government, proceeded to the occupation of all Manchuria. The Chinese appealed to the League, and an international crisis resulted.

The United States by no means stood aloof on this occasion. Secretary Stimson appealed to Geneva to use all the authority within its competence to bring about the peaceful solution of the dispute. He permitted and encouraged the presence of an American member on the famous Lytton investigating commission. On at least two occasions, he suggested that an economic boycott be applied against Japan (though without committing the American government to active participation in such a boycott). He evolved, and secured League acceptance of the so-called Stimson doctrine, by which it was agreed not to recognize as legal or binding any situation created by the violence of the régime in Tokyo. But all these steps taken together were wholly inadequate; they did not prevent the establishment of the puppet kingdom of Manchukuo, under Japanese protectorate, or put an end to the plans of the militarists. American diplomacy sought in vain for a way of making its will prevail that involved no sacrifice and required the facing of no harsh reality.

Still further encouragement no doubt was given to Japanese expansionists by the American attitude towards the Philippines at the close of the Hoover and the opening of the Roosevelt administration. The islands had long desired their independence; and now, by a combination of circumstances, they seemed in a fair way to obtain it. Important American agricultural interests, unfavorably affected by Filipino imports into the United States, combined with labor organizations to support the long agitation of the Filipino leaders for complete self-government. The Hare-Hawes-Cutting Bill, which passed Congress in 1933 over President Hoover's veto, was inacceptable to the inhabitants of the islands. But legislation of similar character was speedily re-enacted, and received the signature of President Roosevelt in March of 1934. There were, it is true, many strings on the grant of independence which was now made. A Filipino commonwealth was to exist till 1946, under a substantial measure of American supervision and protection. The United States did not immediately wash its hands of the islands, or surrender responsibility for their defense. But it seemed to say that it was ready to play a diminishing role in the Orient.

## The Neutrality Acts

The culminating error of American postwar policy, however, came with the enactment of the Neutrality Acts. These extraordinary measures were framed in the years 1935–1937, and received the reluctant, and perhaps we should say the mistaken, signature of the President of the United States. Taking no account of the deeper aspects of the First World War, superficial and shallow in every line, they proceeded on the theory that the way to keep out of the next war was simply to abstain from the various acts which were alleged to have brought us into the previous struggle. Since the munitions traffic, in this view, had been a cause of war, we were not to ship munitions to either belligerent. Since our war trade in general was a cause of war, this trade was to take place only on a cash-and-carry basis, the purchasers acquiring title prior to export and carrying their purchases away on their own ships. Since our war loans, in this view, were a cause of war, we were not to lend money to the belligerents. Since the submarine warfare was a cause of war, we were not to permit our citizens to sail on belligerent merchant vessels, and our own ships were to be excluded from the "war zones" of the contestants.

The passage of legislation such as this in 1937 seems in retrospect an extraordinary act of folly. Adolf Hitler had come to power in 1933. He had already taken Germany out of the League, repudiated the war-guilt clause of the Treaty of Versailles, asserted Germany's liberty of action with regard to rearmament, and occupied the demilitarized region on the west bank of the Rhine. *In the face of all these facts, the American Congress undertook to assure the Fuehrer, by acts of domestic legislation, that if he went to war we would not permit his enemies to be supplied with arms in the United States, that we would not permit them to borrow in the American market, and that we would so conduct ourselves on the high seas as to avoid a conflict with the Reich, even if they chose once more to starve out our erstwhile associate, Great Britain. Could anything have been more fatuous than this?*

## Economic Policy of the United States

As we have already intimated, the troubled times of the thirties were closely connected with the Great Depression. Violent foreign policies sometimes have their roots in economic maladjustment. What was the role of the United States in the twenties in seeking to bring about economic, as distinguished from political, stability? Most certainly a positive effort was made, as, for example, in dealing with the reparations question.

By the signing of a separate peace with Germany, the American government was deprived of an official place on the Reparations Commission, but it was, from the beginning, represented unofficially. When, at the end of 1922, the French, exasperated by what they regarded as Germany's evasion of her responsibilities, proposed to occupy the strategic district of the Ruhr, Mr. Hughes gave vigorous warning of the unwisdom of such action, and proposed that a commission of experts be appointed to deal with the problem. Though his words fell on deaf ears in 1922, they were translated into deeds by 1924. The experts met as Mr. Hughes had wished them to do, and the Dawes Plan for the payment of reparations was the result. When signs appeared that this plan needed revision, it was again an American who gave his name to the settlement. The Young Plan succeeded the Dawes Plan in 1929. In the same period of the twenties, moreover, Americans assisted in the economic rehabilitation of Austria and of Hungary, and played a useful part in the Greco-Turkish transfer of populations mentioned in the preceding chapter, to say nothing of making many smaller contributions.

Yet there were weaknesses in American policy which go to the heart of the problems of the postwar years, and have to do with the approach of new disasters. The American high tariff legislation of the twenties was almost universally condemned by professional economists as wholly inconsistent with the new position of the United States as a creditor nation, with the collection of the war debts (on which the great bulk of American opinion insisted), and with the maximum contribution to European reconstruction. It was a pure piece of self-delusion by which American bankers lent to Germany the sums necessary to the payment of reparations, while high customs duties operated to prevent the repayment of these loans and helped to pave the way for their eventual default. The most elementary maxims of international trade, asserted over and over again by those in a position to speak with authority, were violated lightheartedly and lightheadedly by the men responsible for the determination of governmental action. The temporary recovery of the twenties made it more difficult to enforce the economic truths which needed to be recognized. The generation of Coolidge prosperity, without even being aware of it, was in economic matters animated by no sentiment more respectable than that of the France of Louis XV, "After us the deluge."

The depression of 1929 did not check the unwise direction of American policy. On the contrary, it seemed to accentuate it. Its first result was the Hawley-Smoot tariff bill, one of the most ill-advised and unjustifiable measures in the economic history of the United States. Increasing economic distress only sharpened the preoccupation of the American people with domestic affairs. The bottom of the depression, in 1932, saw, it is true, the virtual ending of the controversy over reparations and war debts, with the complete default of Germany to the victor nations, and the similar default (virtually complete by 1933) of America's associates in the war to America herself. But constructive measures were few and far between. The London Economic Conference, called in 1933 for the restoration of international order, might in any case have been ineffectual, but it was administered a mortal blow by President Roosevelt's refusal (a refusal inconsistent with his previous professions) to take any step towards the stabilization of world currencies. The American departure from the gold standard in the spring of 1933 had the effect of opposing still further barriers to imports into the United States, and accentuating the policy of economic nationalism. The first signs of hope of a wiser course of action were to be found in the Hull reciprocity treaties, patiently negotiated by a Secretary of State who was convinced that a reversal of the trend toward self-sufficiency and economic isolationism was essential to the recovery of all the world, and to the very persistence of our traditional order. *Broadly speaking, however, the American people cannot be said to have learned in the thirties, and very probably have not yet learned in the forties, that the function of world banker which not improbably awaits them in the future, and which, in the interests of a prosperous world society, they might well accept, involves a revision of their views as to tariff protection, and an acceptance of the fundamental maxim that imports are essential to balance the export of capital funds on a large scale.*

## The Retreat from Isolationism

On the whole, as appears from what has been already said, while the American people were not strictly isolationist in their thinking in the postwar years, the emphasis was most certainly in that direction. But the trends which we have been discussing, in both the political and the economic sphere, had begun to be reversed before the outbreak of the Second World War. The policy of the Hull treaties, of reciprocity, was one of the signs of the time. There were indications also of a shift in the international political field.

The denunciation of the treaties of Washington by Japan at the end of 1934, her refusal to renew the naval limitation treaty of London, were followed by increases in American naval appropriations, which reached a new high for time of peace in 1936–1937, and were destined to mount still further with time. More important still was the speech which President Roosevelt made at Chicago, October 5, 1937. This speech does credit to the breadth of his vision, and to his insight into the forces that were operating in the world. On the educational side, indeed, the administration exerted itself quite effectively as the war clouds became more ominous in Europe and in Asia. Again and again the President and his Secretary of State denounced the lawlessness that was more and more evident in Europe and in the Orient. The moral opposition of the United States to the rule of violence was stated vigorously, frankly, and repeatedly, in public utterance, in private diplomatic conversation, and in the diplomatic notes of the period. It was possible, too, for the President to secure from Congress in the session of 1938 naval appropriations which reached the unprecedented and remarkable figure (for those days) of $1,156,000,000. In July the State Department imposed a "moral embargo" on the shipment of planes to belligerents which used them in war against civilians, a pointed thrust at Japan, by this time engaged in a new war of aggression in China.

And in the fall American diplomacy was more active than it had been for some years in seeking to stave off the catastrophe of a European war. In the days before Munich President Roosevelt exerted every effort that he could to maintain the peace; on September 26, he sent a personal message to the heads of the governments of Czechoslovakia, France, Germany and Great Britain urging the continuance of negotiations looking to a settlement of the Sudeten question. Receiving, as was to be expected, a churlish reply from Herr Hitler, he addressed to the German Chancellor a moving personal entreaty that he should hold his hand. On the same day he appealed to Mussolini to use his influence in behalf of a pacific understanding. To what extent his action influenced the final decision for a conference at Munich it is impossible to say. But the President's activities were far from isolationist in spirit, though they were carefully dissociated from any promises of assistance to the democratic nations in the event that war was not avoided.

The peace that came about at Munich was an uneasy peace. There can be little question that in official circles in Washington it was recognized as full of ominous implications for the future. Between October, 1938, and September, 1939, Mr. Roosevelt began to prepare for a change in American foreign policy: for a departure from the tenets of the Neutrality Act of 1937; for a more vigorous role in the Orient. His speech at the opening of the Congressional session of 1939 was no less remarkable than the Chicago speech of 1937. "There comes a time," he declared, "in the affairs of men when they must prepare to defend not their homes alone, but the tenets of faith and humanity on which their churches, their governments and their very civilization are founded. . . . We know what might happen to us if the new philosophy of force were to encompass the other continents and invade our own. We, no more than other nations, can afford to be surrounded by the enemies of our faith and our humanity. The world has grown so small and weapons of attack so swift that no nation can be safe in its will to peace so long as any other single powerful nation refuses to settle its grievances at the council table. . . . In our foreign relations we have learned from the past what not to do. From new wars we have learned what we must do. We have learned that effective timing of defense and the distant points from which attacks may be launched are completely different from what they were twenty years ago. We have learned that survival cannot be guaranteed after the attack begins—for there is a new range and speed to offense. We have learned that long before any overt military act aggression begins with preliminaries of propaganda, subsidized penetration, the loosening of ties of good will, the stirring of prejudice and the incitement to disunion."

Nor did the President confine himself to mere generalization. He recommended the stepping-up of defense appropriations, and in the message just quoted expressed the opinion that the neutrality legislation of 1937 might operate unevenly, might "actually give aid to an aggressor and deny it to the victim"—a hint looking to the repeal of the embargo on the arms traffic that had been incorporated in the statute of less than two years before.

The German occupation of Prague in March of 1939, the Italian invasion of Albania in early April, prompted Mr. Roosevelt to further diplomatic maneuver in the interests of peace, and the education of the American people. On the fourteenth of April he despatched a long appeal to Hitler and Mussolini urging that they give assurances of their peaceable intentions to some thirty nations, mentioned by name; and indicating that if such pledges of nonaggression were received, he would seek similar pledges from each of the nations concerned. From Italy he received no answer whatsoever. The Fuehrer in a brilliantly deceptive speech turned the edge of his proposals, denying that any ambitious enterprises were afoot, and declaring that Germany's neighbors had themselves assured the Reich that they felt quite comfortable in the presence of German armament. The President appeared for the moment checkmated. Yet it may be that his action gave pause to the Axis powers for a little, and that it was not without effect upon the development of American opinion.

By July the administration was ready to go further. By this time the Polish crisis was looming on the horizon; and in view of the pledges given by France and Great Britain to Poland, it was reasonably clear that action by Germany would mean a general European war. Accordingly, Roosevelt urged more insistently than before the repeal of the arms embargo. His proposals were extremely moderate; they not only left most of the neutrality legislation intact, they actually strengthened its provisions with regard to cash and carry — that is, to the acquisition of title to all war materials by the belligerent before shipment from the United States; but they were nonetheless thrust aside by the Congressional leaders in a conference held on the eighteenth of July. It was on this famous occasion that Senator Borah, with an effrontery and complacency so magnificent as to merit commemoration, informed the Secretary of State of the United States that his (Borah's) sources of information were superior to those of the Department itself.

Senator Borah did not stand alone. At the Capitol there seemed to be no real understanding of the imminence of danger. Events marched on; the war clouds loomed thicker and more menacing than ever; on August 24, repeating his tactics of September, 1938, the President appealed to Hitler, to Mussolini, and to President Moszicki of Poland, to bend their utmost energies to the avoidance of war; and receiving a favorable answer from the last of these, he sent next day a special appeal to the German Chancellor. But there was, after all, no will to peace in Berlin; on September first the German armies entered Poland, and once again the nations stood at Armageddon.

In the affairs of the Orient, too, the administration by the end of 1938 began to step up its tone. The sharpest protest yet launched at the conduct of the Japanese in China was delivered on December 31, 1938; at the same time a loan was extended to the hard-pressed government at Chungking which, though stated to be merely commercial in character, could hardly fail to encourage Chinese resistance to Nippon and aid in Chinese prosecution of the war. A much more ominous move was taken in July of 1939. When Senator Vandenberg introduced a resolution looking to the termination of the commercial treaty of 1911 with Japan, the administration acted promptly in giving notice of such termination, and the way was cleared for retaliatory action in the Orient against the overweening power of the militarists. The period of moral homilies was thus indicated as drawing to an end; the acquiescence of the United States in Japanese imperialism could no longer be taken for granted, any more than the acquiescence of the United States in the onward march of Adolf Hitler. *When the German armies entered Poland, the American people had been prepared by their government infinitely better than in 1914, to take such action as might be appropriate to the upholding of their interests and their ideals in Europe and the Far East alike. They were surely much less "isolationist" at the later date than at the earlier.*

## American Relations with Great Britain

Before bringing this chapter to an end, there is one other aspect of the period that must be considered. Just as in 1914 the

American people were prepared to weigh the belligerents in different scales, so were they also in 1939. This fact will become clear if we examine American relations with Great Britain and with Germany in the years between Versailles and the renewed outbreak of war.

In the year 1914, we have already seen, the United States had enjoyed more than a decade of excellent relations with Great Britain. With Germany, on the other hand, there had been irritations and causes of suspicion; the prejudice of the Americans was firmly set in favor of one and against the other of these two great nations. The same situation, it need hardly be said, reproduced itself in 1939, though the difference is even sharper than it had been twenty-five years before.

One factor in good relations between the British and American peoples was the change that took place in Ireland. The establishment of the Irish Free State in 1921 removed, or at any rate immensely diminished, one great source of friction. Though there were many Irishmen, it is true, who were slow to forget what they deemed with reason to be the harsh and selfish attitude of England toward Ireland, and though the cutting off of Northern Ireland from the Free State left an irritating problem still unsettled, there could hardly be the same antagonism which existed in the earlier period.

The concession of freedom to Ireland, however, was after all wise statesmanship in itself, and cannot be said to have been made primarily to gratify American opinion. It was otherwise with some of the steps which followed. At the Washington Naval Conference Great Britain made the substantial concession of agreeing to parity for the United States in capital ships and aircraft carriers; and influenced partly by American and partly by Dominion opinion, she substituted for her alliance with Japan (always unpopular in the United States) the so-called Four-Power Pact, which was, after all, a much looser type of compact. Forced to choose between her Oriental ally and her transatlantic friend, in a sense she made her election in favor of the latter. Her choice was significant, and perhaps it had something to do with the gradual gravitation of Japan towards new associations and new alliances.

There were new concessions just around the corner. In 1923 Great Britain funded her war debt to the United States; she was the first of the great nations to do so and she received the least favorable terms of any of America's debtors. Four years later, it is true, when called upon by the American government in the name of "parity" to reduce her naval armaments beyond the levels of 1922, and in particular to cut down her cruiser strength, Great Britain balked; the then First Lord of the Admiralty, Mr. Winston Spencer Churchill, was largely responsible for this fact, and the view that he then took seems to have much to commend it today, when the needs of a large navy are so apparent; but in 1929, when a Labour government came into power, the British attitude changed; and at the London Conference British naval needs were in part adjusted (some would say sacrificed) to meet the views of the United States. If there were in this period sources of irritation, such as the British rubber monopoly in the East Indies, it is fair to say that they were purely minor; and both the American and the British governments reacted in similar fashion — in similar shortsighted fashion, shall we say — to the plaints of France with regard to the necessity for a more solid edifice of European security. The cordiality of the twenties was for a little while interrupted by the depression; the British departure from gold in 1931 was not favorably regarded in the United States; the protectionist policy within the Empire, adopted by the Ottawa Imperial Conference of 1932, was also unfavorable to American interests (though the nation which had enacted the Hawley-Smoot tariff bill certainly had no reason to complain) and the rough and sudden manner in which President Roosevelt tipped over the hopes of currency stabilization at the time of the London Economic Conference was also no great contribution to the close association of the two nations. But before long, the two governments came to an agreement on the relationship of dollar and pound in terms of gold; the protectionist wave in the United States receded with the negotiation of the Hull reciprocity treaties; and no really serious issues vexed the relationships of the British and American governments in the middle thirties. There were Americans, of course, who wondered at the extraordinary complacency of British policy in the face of German rearmament; there were an increasing number who were critical of that policy in even larger terms — who deprecated the fiasco of sanctions against Italy in the Ethiopian matter; who condemned the farce of nonintervention by means of which Spain was delivered over to the Fascists, with the connivance of France and of Great Britain; who were horrified at Munich, and the abandonment of Czechoslovakia. But it ill behooved any citizen of the United States, when the flood of isolationist sentiment was still high at home, to criticize too harshly the British for their errors, obvious as these were to become; and as the reaction against isolationism set in, it was registered in the action of the American administration with regard to Britain. It was a remarkable and unprecedented move which President Roosevelt made in 1938 when he brought Canada within the scope of the Monroe Doctrine; reciprocity agreements with both Canada and Great Britain had been concluded before the outbreak of war; and, as we have already seen, the trend of the President's diplomacy in 1939 was frankly directed towards assisting the democracies, and pillorying the totalitarian states. All in all, there could be little doubt where American favor would lie if the peace of Europe was again broken.

## American Relations with Germany

The course of American public opinion with regard to Germany ran a somewhat different course, and had in 1939 reached a pitch of genuine antagonism. There was plenty of feeling in the twenties which regarded the Treaty of Versailles as unduly harsh; public sentiment condemned the attempt of France to extract reparations from Germany by the occupation of the Ruhr; and, as in Britain, many good and somewhat naïve people committed themselves to the idea of "revision." The outpouring of loans to Germany was partly sustained by the feeling that here was a wonderful country which ought to be assisted along the pathway of recovery; and the ease with which these loans were absorbed owed something — one cannot say how much — to the same kind of feeling. But with the advent of Adolf Hitler to power the popular attitude began to change. The wisest and best-informed men had no illusions about the new régime from the first; before long the Germans repudiated their indebtedness to the United States and this was naturally resented; the shameless agitation of the German *Bund* was annoying, if futile; and worse than all of these, the persecution of the Jews affronted the American sense of fair play, and alienated a substantial element in our population which was not without influence on public opinion through the medium of the press, the movies, and the radio. For a long time, it is true, the public mood was one of moral protest, not in any sense of belligerency. But the increasing violence of Hitler produced its effect; and the tension of 1938 produced a strong impact upon American opinion. In December of that year a *Fortune* poll revealed the fact that 56 per cent of the American people thought that the United States ought to join with the European democracies in case they were involved in war with Germany. There was certainly a far more explosive situation, so far as Germany was concerned, in 1939 than in 1914.

The additional factor of tension at the later of these two dates, it hardly needs to be said, was the tension with Japan. There were Americans at this period, including the distinguished publicist, Mr. Walter Lippmann, who deprecated the drift of affairs, on the understandable ground that it was unfortunate to be moving towards a quarrel in both oceans and both hemispheres at once; but the popular resentment at Japanese policy in China was not to be controlled by such considerations, nor was the policy of the administration. As we have already seen, assistance was given to China; American principles and policies in the Far East were continuously reasserted; the denunciation of the commercial treaty of 1911 paved the way for measures of economic pressure against Nippon. By the summer of 1939 80 per cent of Americans appeared to favor an embargo against the Island Empire; and the illusion persisted widely (to be refuted by events in 1941) that such an embargo would bring the Japanese militarists to terms.

## Summary

*What, indeed, was the meaning of all this? Put in a nutshell, the developments which we have traced so hastily meant just one thing. They meant that the American people could not and would not remain indifferent to what went on in other parts of the world. It ought by now to be clear that it is pure theory to imagine that it can be otherwise. We do not need to argue; we do not need to explain. The plain and inescapable fact is that Americans feel a responsibility for what goes on outside their borders; the only debatable question is as to the means by which this responsibility shall be discharged.*

*If we compare 1939 with 1914, one thing is clear. Despite*

*American reluctance to make commitments in this intermediate period, by the end of it, the interest of the United States in the politics of Europe and Asia was obviously much greater than it had been a quarter of a century before. The passage of the years of war and peace had not been without effect; the scope of American thought had widened with time; and the scale of American action was to be widened in its turn. While the future was still obscure, it might have been, indeed it was, foreseen by those in the best situation to judge. It is a fact to bear in memory that in October of 1937 Franklin D. Roosevelt had warned the American people that they would not escape, if the nations sounded once again the trumpets of battle.*

# VI

## The Years of Nonbelligerency, 1914 and 1939

*The war of 1939 began with American opinion highly favorable to the democratic nations. With the fall of France, the conviction mounted that an issue of security was involved. At the same time the aggressive action of Japan in the East, and especially the alliance with the Axis on September 27, 1940, increased the tension of American-Japanese relations. American policy, backed by majority sentiment, moved towards franker and fuller assistance to Britain, and towards clearer opposition to the imperialism of Tokyo. The final challenge came from the militarist nations, with the attack on Pearl Harbor and the declarations of war by Germany and Italy on the United States. Once again, it had been demonstrated that a general world conflagration inevitably affected the views of the American people and involved them within its scope.*

### General Considerations

In the World War of 1914–1918 American public opinion was, at the beginning, biased, but not bellicose. A long tradition suggested the maintenance of American neutrality; the policy of the Wilson administration reflected this fact. The President certainly did not think at the outset in terms of involvement in the struggle; on the contrary, it was his object to keep out of it, and his hope to mediate between the two groups of belligerents and bring about peace. In practice the scales were not held even between the Entente Powers and the Central Empires. A subtle partiality pervaded American policy, dictated the strong stand which was taken against the submarine warfare, and eventually contributed to our entry into the war itself. But this partiality related to the maintenance of neutral rights and President Wilson, as the leader of the American people, based his foreign policy on this fundamental principle. As time went on, it is true, the President's vision broadened. By the end of 1915 he was coming to the view that the United States must participate, at the end of the struggle, in some general association of the nations for the maintenance of peace; and he gave frank expression to this view in his speech of the twenty-seventh of May, 1916. But it was not until after our actual entrance into the war that Wilson even touched upon the question of American security, that he even hinted at the hypothesis that German militarism constituted a threat to the tranquillity, perhaps to the physical safety, of the United States itself. There are evidences that he had some inkling of this idea much earlier; the reader will remember his talk with Cecil Spring-Rice in September of 1914. But before our entrance into the war he gave it no official expression; and in this respect he was certainly representative of a very large body of American opinion.

By contrast, President Roosevelt had begun to make it clear in his public utterances, some time before the German armies entered Poland in September of 1939, that the outbreak of a general European war could not be regarded with indifference by the United States; and in the period of nonbelligerency, from September, 1939 to December, 1941, he more and more boldly proclaimed his conviction that the triumph of German militarism constituted a positive threat to the vital interests of the American people. On this hypothesis he may fairly be said to have acted; on occasion he was in advance of American opinion; at the same time he interpreted it, sometimes leading, sometimes following, never cutting himself off from it. As we shall see, however, there was at all times substantial opposition to the drift of his policy, opposition based on the strongly pacific temper of the American people, on the widely held opinion that no transatlantic or transpacific power could seriously threaten the American continents, on reluctance to turn from a program of domestic reconstruction to a program that was deemed one of adventure in the field of foreign affairs. Just as in 1914–1917 American opinion was divided, so it was divided between 1939 and 1941; and in the one case, as in the other, it may well be doubted whether anything less than a decisive act of aggression on the part of our enemies would have actually involved the United States in war.

## Roosevelt's Policy until the Collapse of France

In September of 1939, at the beginning of the Second World War, there was very general reprobation of Nazi Germany, a widespread sympathy with Great Britain, but by no means a militant attitude, or a willingness to make great sacrifices in the cause of the Allies. Most Americans assumed at the outset of the struggle (doubtless influenced by their sympathies and predilections) that the democratic nations would surely win; there was still a general feeling that the entry into the last war had been a mistake; that the most that was necessary was to provide France and Great Britain with the materials for victory. On this latter question the President, as we have seen, had already expressed himself in January, and more emphatically and concretely in July; and just after the outbreak of war a poll of the Institute of Public Opinion showed that 57 per cent of the people of the United States were in favor of the modification of the Neutrality Act to permit the purchase of war materials in the United States.

Interpreting the majority feeling, Mr. Roosevelt on September 21 sent a message to Congress demanding the modification of the legislation of 1937. He laid the emphasis not on getting into, but on keeping out of, war; he declared the embargo provisions of two years to be "wholly inconsistent with ancient precepts of the law of nations"; he pointed out the inconsistency of permitting the shipment of unprocessed materials to the Allies, but not of finished products of war; he frankly expressed his regret that he had signed the previous enactment. He suggested that in other respects the neutrality laws be strengthened, not weakened.

His recommendations touched off a partisan battle. The Democrats rallied to the support of the President with very few exceptions; the Republicans, on the other hand, were for the most part aligned in opposition. In the Senate the line was less sharply drawn; yet essentially the same situation existed. The legislation of the fall of 1939 proved to be highly controversial.

In retrospect, the opposition to the President may appear factious and reprehensible. It ought not to. It cannot be stated too often that partisanship in foreign policy in the United States is the indication of a simple and important fact, the fact that the country has not made up its mind; it is normal for the party out of power to adopt a critical attitude towards those in authority; and while in looking back it may be true that the attitude assumed by the mass of Republicans in Congress was lacking in vision and in breadth, we need to remember that many things that are clear today were not clear four years ago. In the then prevailing state of the public mind the division upon the repeal of the arms embargo is neither surprising nor necessarily to be condemned. At the end of 1939 the dominant opinion of the nation still desired that the United States stay out of the war; the vote against the administration reflected, in some measure, this important fact.

The assumptions of the fall of 1939, on the one side and on the other, were both framed in the assurance that the democratic nations would win the war. This comfortable view could be indulged in during the inactive winter of 1940. But it was bound to be revised in the light of the tragic events of the succeeding spring. For in April the Germans launched their attack on Norway; in May they unleashed the great offensive in the West, trampling Belgium and Holland underfoot; in June they brought the French armies to defeat, and emerged the conquerors of Western Europe. Never has a more dramatic alteration of the international situation taken place; and with it America faced the possibility not only of a German domination of the Continent, but of a possible collapse of Britain as well. True, the hapless government of Neville Chamberlain was overthrown; a great leader in the person of Winston Churchill took the helm; but the peril in which England stood was greater than at any period in modern history, and the destruction of Britain implied a drastic change in the whole international scheme.

## Aid to the Democracies

Once again the President reflected with fidelity, in many respects, the changing mood of the American people. Again and again he had sounded the note of moral condemnation of the methods of Hitlerian Germany. Now he stressed the element of national security for the United States. In his speech before the Eighth Pan-American Scientific Congress on May 10, 1940, he alluded to the "mistaken idea" that "a distance of several thousand miles from Europe gave to us some form of mystic immunity which could never be violated."

Speaking in terms of time-tables, he went on, "every acre—every hectare—in all the Americas from the Arctic to the Antarctic is closer to the homes of modern conquerors and the scenes of attack in Europe than was the case in historic efforts to dominate the world in bygone centuries." In a message to Congress calling for additional appropriations for national defense, on the sixteenth of May, he emphasized this thought still further. In a radio speech ten days later he spoke frankly of the "futility" of the idea that "we could maintain our physical safety by retiring within our Continental boundaries." And on June 10, in one of the most famous of his utterances, that at Charlottesville, Virginia, with the news of the French collapse and of the Italian entry into the war staring the country in the face, he went even further. "Let us not hesitate—all of us—to proclaim certain truths. Overwhelmingly we, as a nation—and this applies to all the other American nations—are convinced that military and naval victory for the gods of force and hate would endanger the institutions of democracy in the Western world. . . . On this tenth day of June, 1940, in this University founded by the first great American teacher of democracy, we send forth our prayers and our hopes to those beyond the seas who are maintaining with magnificent valor the battle for freedom. In our unity, our American unity, we will pursue two obvious and simultaneous courses: we will extend to the opponents of force the material resources of the nation and at the same time we will harness and speed up the use of those resources in order that we ourselves in the Americas may have equipment and training equal to the task of any emergency and every defense." A clearer and sharper challenge to the American people to face the new facts, the new situation, could hardly have been imagined.

There were ample evidences that the President had not misinterpreted the attitude of the American people. By substantial majorities the Congress enacted a Selective Service Law, the first selective service law in time of peace. In June and July it appropriated no less than $10,000,000,000 for national defense. At the Republican Nominating Convention which met at the end of June, the candidate of the "isolationists," and those candidates whose position was equivocal or doubtful, were swept aside. In a popular movement which has its closest parallel in the Democratic Nominating Convention of 1912 (the convention which nominated Woodrow Wilson), the Republicans turned aside from the practised players of the game to select as their candidate Wendell Willkie, whose sincere conviction on the dangers of the time squared with those of the President himself. By one of the happiest developments in our political history, the country was spared a divisive and disruptive debate on foreign policy at a time when unity was essential to effective action.

In the United States an administration has often been hampered in taking effective action in the field of foreign affairs in the months just before a Presidential election. No such inertia prevailed in the summer of 1940. The Charlottesville speech was no pussyfooting declaration of a Mr. Facing-both-ways. In the summer the President took a bold and ingenious step to supplement it. On September 3 there was announced the famous destroyer-bases deal, by which fifty vessels, politely described as overage, were handed over to hard-pressed Britain in exchange for the donation to the United States of certain bases in Newfoundland and in Bermuda, and the lease of several others in the region of the Caribbean. The step was widely applauded; and the Republican candidate for the Presidency himself expressed his approval, though he was critical of the manner in which Mr. Roosevelt had acted — without consultation with the legislative body.

## Latin America and the Orient

The destroyer-bases deal was by no means the only step taken by the administration to strengthen the American position. A Pan-American Conference meeting at Havana drew up plans for the provisional occupation and "collective trusteeship" of colonies in the American hemisphere left derelict by Nazi victory; steps were taken in common looking to the exchange of information on Axis propaganda; an Inter-American Financial and Advisory Committee, established the preceding year, was enlarged and authorized to study special phases of the problem of trade; the capital of the Export-Import Bank was increased.

At the same time the administration made increasingly clear its position in the Far East. Since the first loan to China in 1938, it had gradually strengthened its forces in the Pacific. The bulk of the American fleet lay in these waters; naval and air bases were begun at many points where they might be essential to defense — at Midway and Wake, at Dutch Harbor in the Aleutians; in December of 1939 the "moral embargo" of the summer of 1938 was extended; in January the commercial treaty of 1911 was denounced. On April 17, 1940, Secretary Hull warned the Japanese in no uncertain terms of American interest in the Dutch East Indies; on July 26, the administration placed the export of petroleum and scrap iron under licensing control; a week later it banned the export of aviation gasoline. By measures of increasing rigor it sought to express American displeasure with Japanese policy.

Of the tenor of that policy there could not now be the slightest doubt. The Japanese militarists were more and more securely installed in power as time went on. Internally, the limitations placed upon their power by the Diet were more and more overridden; and in July, 1940, the advent of the cabinet of Prince Konoye, and the appointment of Yosuke Matsuoka as Foreign Minister, were followed by a declaration describing Japan's objective as a "new order for Greater East Asia," a phrase which hardly bothered to conceal the mounting ambitions and territorial appetites of the reigning elements in Tokyo. Before another two months had gone by, moreover, a step was taken that was even more decisive, so far as the United States was concerned; on September 27, 1940, the Japanese made their fateful alliance with the Axis powers, and bound themselves to enter the war on the side of Germany and Italy in the event that America cast its weight into the European balance. The freedom of action of the American government, then, was to be decided upon not in Washington, not by the chosen leaders of the American people, but by a group of military fanatics on the other side of the Pacific. Does it not seem strange today that the decision of September 27, 1940, aroused no great storm of resentment on this side of the water?

## Lend-Lease

The election of 1940 was held under circumstances increasingly ominous for the peace of the United States and of the world. The predatory nations had united, they had publicly solemnized their union; and against them in arms, and in arms against only one of them, was Great Britain alone. Yet American opinion was by no means militant; the speeches of both candidates, sometimes evasive, and disposed to pledge peace while faced with an increasing menace, reflected this temper. Like many individuals in many different sets of circumstances, the American people in 1940 really wanted certain contradictory and mutually incompatible things; they wanted to keep out of war, and they also wanted the Nazis to be defeated. It was only a very small proportion of them who had the clarity of vision to see that they could not have one without the other.

By November, 1940, however, the sentiment for giving substantial aid to the Allies had grown to significant proportions. In the *Fortune* poll of that month 15.9 per cent of those interrogated wished the United States to declare itself an ally of Great Britain and send supplies and equipment and even men if necessary; 41 per cent wished to do all these things except to send men. In other words, more than a majority were in favor of a wide measure of aid. These figures were a striking advance over those of August in a poll taken by the same magazine. They indicated a drift of which the President was prompt to take advantage.

When the new Congress met, therefore, in January, 1941, Mr. Roosevelt came forward with the proposals that are known as lend-lease. Once again he stressed the thesis that had now become a central part of his thinking. "In times like these it is immature — and incidentally untrue — for anybody to brag that an unprepared America, single-handed, and with one hand tied behind its back, can hold off the whole world. No realistic American can expect from a dictator's peace international generosity, or return of true independence, or world disarmament, or freedom of expression, or freedom of religion — or even good business. Such a peace would bring no security for us or for our neighbors. . . . There is much loose talk of our immunity from immediate and direct invasion from across the seas. Obviously, so long as the British navy retains its power, no such danger exists. Even if there were no British navy, it is not probable that any enemy would be stupid enough to attack us by landing troops in the United States from across thousands of miles of ocean, unless it had acquired strategic bases from which to operate. . . . The first phase of the invasion of this hemisphere would not be the landing of regular troops. The necessary strategic points would be occupied by secret agents and their dupes — and great numbers of them are already here, and in Latin America. As long as the aggressor nations maintain the offensive, they — not we — will choose the time and the place and the method of their attack. That is why the future of all American republics is today in serious danger."

The President went on to declare that the answer to this peril lay in furnishing the maximum aid to Britain and her allies in her struggle against the Nazis. "They do not need man-power. They do need billions of dollars' worth of the weapons of defense. The time is near when they will not be able to pay for them in ready cash. We cannot and will not tell them that they must surrender, merely because of present inability to pay for the weapons which we know they must have. I do not recommend that we make them a loan of dollars with which to pay for these weapons — a loan to be repaid in dollars. I recommend that we make it possible for those nations to continue to obtain war materials in the United States, fitting their orders into our own program. . . . Let us say to the democracies: 'We Americans are vitally concerned in your defense of freedom. We are putting forth our energies, our resources and our organizing powers to give you the strength to regain and maintain a free world. We shall send you in ever-increasing numbers ships, planes, tanks, guns. This is our purpose and our pledge.' "

The President's proposal in the message of January 6, 1941, may fairly be said to be unprecedented in modern history. It would have been inconceivable in the climate of opinion of 1914–1917 or of 1939–1940. Neutrality was a legal and philosophical idea that had strong roots in the thoughts of the nineteenth and early twentieth century. America herself had powerfully contributed to the growth of that idea. It was part of the warp and woof of the thinking of the time. The Roosevelt proposal of January, 1941, represented a completely different conception. It was a conception which would have brought joy to the heart of Woodrow Wilson if he had been alive to see it flower. It was the conception that aggression was immoral, that there was no difficulty about identifying it (as some of the legalistic minds of the earlier period would have contended), and that the duty of a great and powerful nation was to aid in opposing it, and seeing it frustrated. It was the conception of a League to Enforce Peace, with the accent on the word *Enforce*. It was the revival, in more concrete, more realistic and more sweeping form of the ideas which had been in the air, but which had not got themselves accepted by the American people, a quarter of a century before.

Would it now be accepted? The answer was to be given in the great debate—and it was a great debate—that took place on the Lend-Lease Bill, H.R. 1776, in the winter months of this momentous year. There were those who complained of the slowness of our constitutional processes at this time. But the issues were of the first order of importance, and it was only fitting that they should be solemnly and fully discussed by the representatives of the American people. In this debate, as in that of the fall of 1939, there were still many evidences of partisanship—evidences, as has been said, of the natural division of American opinion. But the majorities for the legislation sought by the President were in the last analysis impressive; in the House the vote was 317 to 171; in the Senate it was 60 to 31. There was still a partisan flavor to the vote, but 35 Republicans voted for the bill in the House, and 10 in the Senate. Lend-lease was not finagled through Congress; it represented the mature and deliberate judgment of our national legislature.

Yet it is doubtful if all those who supported it were fully aware of its possible consequences. It is very human to want what one wants without facing consequences. It was easy to approve of aid to Britain if it involved no sacrifices; but could aid be given without sacrifice? The German submarines, long before this, had been ranging the Atlantic; were we now to stand by and watch them sink the cargoes which we were consigning to the democracies abroad? The question was of fundamental importance; and it arose almost as soon as the lend-lease enactment received the President's signature.

The administration answered it with effective action. American naval and air forces were sent to patrol the Atlantic; on April 9, an agreement was signed with the Danish Minister at Washington (who was naturally disavowed by the captive government at Copenhagen) by which the United States was permitted to occupy Greenland; three months later American troops occupied Iceland; while in a widely different area advantage was taken of the favorable turn of military events to declare the southern area of the Red Sea no longer a combat zone, and therefore accessible to American shipping. These steps were all consistent with the newly declared policy of the United States; they were taken by the President acting on his own authority as Commander in Chief of the Army and Navy; and they received the support of a substantial body of public opinion.

## Vichy

But lend-lease was not the only expression of American diplomatic activity in the course of the first half of 1941. Most important was the attitude of the administration with regard to the French régime which had been set up at Vichy. This government, it ought to be understood, was, from a strictly legal point of view, the successor of the Third Republic; it was, indeed, the only constituted government; and what was practically more important, it retained control of the French fleet and the French colonies. It was by no means certain in 1940 and 1941 that it would sink into the degrading subservience to Germany which was later to be true of it; and indeed before the year was out, the ousting by Marshal Pétain of the sinister Pierre Laval, and the appointment of Admiral Darlan as his first minister and possible successor, while affording no reason for any particular trustful relationship, did seem to indicate a drift away from the policy of unreserved collaboration with Germany. While the facts of the matter are not and cannot be fully known now, it seems probable that at the end of 1940 the French Chief of State still hoped to maintain a measure of independence against the conqueror.

Taking all these facts into consideration, the administration decided to try to do business with the Vichy régime. It was not until after the election that a regularly accredited representative, Admiral Leahy, was sent to France; but from the time of the armistice we had an American chargé there, Mr. Robert Murphy. This latter official enjoyed the good graces of both Pétain and General Weygand, the French proconsul in North Africa. In February of 1941 it proved possible to negotiate an agreement by which the United States would make available a certain amount of food and other materials for the North African colonies; in exchange, American control officers were to be admitted to these provinces, and General Weygand was to hold Germany and Italy strictly to the terms of the armistice. Though it is difficult to believe that foresight went so far as to take into consideration the possibility of American landings twenty-two months later, no diplomatic arrangement of the pre-war period brought richer dividends to the United States, or has had more to do with the successful prosecution of the war.

The story of Admiral Leahy's mission to Vichy remains to be written; it cannot now be told in detail. But the outline is clear. The spring of 1941 was a threatening period, so far as

French relations with Germany were concerned; once more it seemed as if the aged Marshal Pétain and his fugleman Admiral Darlan were going to capitulate before Hitler. On the fourth of May a pledge was secured from the Chief of State that France would not exceed the armistice terms in Germany's favor. But the next week Darlan visited Berchtesgaden; and at the same time, so it was alleged, thirty German planes reached Iraq, where an anti-British movement was under way, fourteen of them having grounded in Syria, which was under French control. Much concerned at the trend of events, President Roosevelt, on the fifteenth, broadcast to France by short wave, urging loyalty to the American tie and to her own tradition; Secretary Hull, ten days later, held a frank conference with Mr. Henry-Haye, the Vichy Minister to the United States, in which he warned of the consequences of new concessions to Hitler; on the fifth of June he broadcast to the French people. For a time it seemed as if the battle were going against the administration; but two events intervened. General Weygand, loyal to the agreement with the United States, exerted all his influence to keep Vichy from complete surrender to Germany; and in the second place, on the twenty-second of June, the Nazi régime began its ill-fated invasion of Russia, relieving the pressure on the unhappy government of Marshal Pétain.

## Aid to Russia

For this latter move, the most dramatic and the most momentous of the entire war, the government of the United States had not been ill prepared. Naturally, American sentiment towards Russia had not been cordial after the appeasement pact with Germany in 1939. It was rendered no more so by the Russian hostilities with Finland, or by the Russian acquisition of the Baltic provinces in the spring of 1940. But the collapse of France tended to bring the two governments nearer together; and as early as January, 1941, Undersecretary of State Welles had told Constantine Oumansky, the Russian Ambassador, that he had reliable information that Germany was planning to attack the Soviet Union. Moscow asked and subsequently received confirmatory evidence of the facts alleged. By June official tension had decidedly relaxed; and the outbreak of the war in Eastern Europe was speedily followed by the special mission of the President's trusted adviser, Mr. Harry Hopkins, to Moscow. In an epoch-making conference, the bases were laid for lend-lease aid to Russia on a grandiose scale; and before fall a special Anglo-American delegation had gone over the ground in detail, and determined upon the volume and type of supplies which were to be provided the government of Joseph Stalin. The action of the United States was steadily widening, its role becoming increasingly important in the struggle against the totalitarian states.

### The Atlantic Charter

In the summer of 1941, moreover, President Roosevelt and Winston Churchill met together off the coast of Newfoundland, and there drew up the remarkable document known as the Atlantic Charter. In every war, along with the severely practical problems which it raises, there is an effort, probably a necessary and inevitable effort, to state its purpose in ideal and widely persuasive terms. There is always danger in such a course, for it is easy to arouse false expectations and over-grandiose dreams for the future. There had been something of this, as we have seen, in the Wilsonian efforts of 1917 and 1918. But, on the other hand, the instinct to give to a great national effort the character of a crusade for righteousness and peace is strong in the Anglo-Saxon peoples; and perhaps it may fairly be said that it is better to fix a high standard to live up to, even if one fails, than never to fix a standard at all. At any rate, however one may view the matter, this is precisely what the Atlantic Charter does. The language is cautious, and lays down no absolute prescriptions. What is suggested is not a specific program, a blueprint of the future. The President and the Prime Minister "deem it right to make known certain common principles of the national policies of their respective countries on which they base their hopes for a better future for the world." These principles are treated as already existing; they are not declared for the first time. They are compressed as follows: They look first of all to the liberation of the peoples of Europe, and to territorial settlements in accordance with "the freely expressed wishes of the peoples concerned"; they declare that the two countries concerned "seek no aggrandizement, territorial or other"; they call for freer trade and "the enjoyment by all states, great and small, victor or vanquished, of access on equal terms to the trade and to the raw materials of the world which are needed for their economic prosperity; they speak of "collaboration between all nations" in the interests of improved economic conditions for all; and they look forward to a peace in the future in which men "may live in safety and traverse the high seas and oceans without hindrance." Finally, they declare that the disarmament of aggressor nations is a condition precedent to peace.

It may be worth while to restate these propositions in somewhat more concrete language. They implied, first of all, in their renunciation of aggrandizement, some kind of international control of the substantial territories which will come, or have come, into the hands of the democracies as the result of the war; they implied the redrawing of the map of Europe on the principle of self-determination which Woodrow Wilson sought to apply in 1919; they implied lower tariffs, "with due respect for . . . existing obligations," as their language reads;

they implied the creation of machinery to keep Germany and Japan disarmed, "pending the establishment of a wider and permanent system of general security."

The declaration of the Atlantic Charter naturally invites comparison with the Fourteen Points of twenty-three years before. In the light of our experience then, we should be a little simple-minded if we expected the Churchill-Roosevelt program to be translated instantaneously into reality at the end of the present war. There is nothing more dangerous for any of us than to indulge the hope of an early millennium. The President and the Prime Minister saw this themselves. They were less concrete and specific than President Wilson, wisely so; and they expressed "their hopes for a better future," not a program that was to be realized overnight. Even so, they may have stored up troubles for themselves in the days ahead, in particular with regard to the principle of self-determination. We have already seen how great are the difficulties which the application of this principle involves.

Of one aspect of the Atlantic Charter, however, it is possible to speak with definiteness. It was framed, be it emphasized, four months before the entry of the United States into the war. It was, therefore, we may fairly say, an act of remarkable audacity on the part of the President of the United States; the identification of American and British policy, underlined by the lend-lease legislation of the winter of 1941, was carried to still greater length in the August manifesto. For better or for worse, two great and kindred nations took their stand side by side in proclaiming certain fundamental principles for the future.

## The Mounting Crisis with Germany

In this same summer of 1941, however, American opinion continued to be much divided and by no means unanimously prepared to follow the lead of the President. Legislation came before Congress at just this time looking to the extension for a period of eighteen months of the service of those who had been already called to the colors; it met with the most severe opposition in Congress; and in the form desired by the military authorities it actually passed the House of Representatives by a majority of one, by 203 to 202. Of the Republican members voting, 133 out of 154 declined to support the administration, and they were joined by no less than 65 Democrats, the largest number yet found in opposition. It is possible, of course, that a slightly shorter period of service would have rallied a stronger majority; but such a vote, in the face of the demand of the armed services, in the circumstances of the time can indicate only that the American people, or at any rate their representatives, were as yet far from realizing to the full the situation which confronted and would confront them.

The fall, also, held some dramatic developments. It was the strategy of the President to leave to the Nazis the striking of the first blow; during the months since passage of the Lend-Lease Bill American patrols had ranged the Atlantic; American airplanes had signified to British vessels the location of Nazi submarines; but no actual act of force had been committed by the ships or planes of the United States. It was inevitable, of course, that sooner or later some incident would occur; and the incident came when an American warship, which was carrying the mails to Iceland, but which was also giving information as to the position of a German U-boat, was turned upon by the latter, which fired a futile torpedo in its direction. The President promptly declared that hereafter American vessels, when they came into contact with German submarines, would not hesitate to strike the first blow and had been given orders to this effect. By his own act as Commander in Chief of the armed forces he thus began a kind of informal warfare against Germany. No decision made by him was more far-reaching than this; none, it may fairly be said, stretched further his constitutional power. Yet if the policy of lend-lease were sound, it seemed worse than futile to permit the supplies that the United States was sending to Great Britain to be sunk with impunity; and, if there seemed to many persons something a bit disingenuous or, at least, metaphysical in describing all these activities in terms of "defense," it was still true that they followed naturally enough from the lend-lease policy adopted after prolonged debate in the winter of 1941.

A month later the President went further. He recommended to Congress new changes in the neutrality legislation of 1937. In wholly specific terms, he asked authority to arm the merchant vessels of the United States. In language almost as definite, he at the same time indicated his own conviction that it was time to repeal the provision by which American vessels were forbidden to enter certain specified "war zones." He indicated that it would be increasingly necessary, as the lend-lease program proceeded, to "deliver American goods under the American flag." "I say to you solemnly," he declared, "that if Hitler's military plans are brought to successful fulfillment, we Americans shall be forced to fight in defense of our own homes, and our own freedom in a war as costly and as devastating as that which now rages on the Russian front. Hitler has offered a challenge which we as Americans cannot and will not tolerate." It would be difficult to find a parallel for language more bellicose than this on the part of the Chief Executive of a nation which was not yet at war.

Congress was by no means united in support of the Executive. A bill to arm the merchant ships of the United States passed the House of Representatives on October 17 by a vote of 259 to 138; of the opposition, 113 were Republicans. Before the Senate came to a decision on the measure, there were new "incidents" at sea: the United States destroyer *Kearny* was torpedoed on October 18; the *Reuben James* went to the bottom of the ocean on October 30. Acting under the influence of these new events, the Senate went further than the House; it attached to the House bill a provision permitting American ships to enter the waters from which they had been excluded under early legislation. This measure, which gave the President all that he wanted, passed the upper house by a vote of 50 to 27, a very substantial margin; but when it went back to the lower house a bitter fight occurred. The final vote was hardly less than frightening as a symptom of national division; the House accepted the Senate bill by a margin of only eighteen votes, by 212 to 194. This time the Republican opposition rose to 137; and 53 Democrats joined the foes of the administration.

The legislative battle of November, 1941, should not be misunderstood, however, nor should the partisan character of the opposition be overstressed. At the end of 1916, after two and a half years of struggle in Europe, the country still desired peace, and voted Woodrow Wilson back into power because he had striven to preserve it; yet it followed him to war without serious opposition in the spring of 1917. In November, 1941, it was difficult for many sincere and intelligent men to believe that the danger was as great as the President painted it; and it needed a decisive and dramatic act to unify American opinion. That act, we need hardly say, was provided by Hitler's Oriental ally, by the government of Japan. It is necessary for us to go back at this point, and trace the development of our relations with the régime at Tokyo.

## The Crisis with Japan

The treaty of the twenty-seventh of September, 1940, by which the Japanese were linked with the Axis powers could hardly be otherwise regarded than as a threat to the diplomatic freedom of action of the United States. Within two weeks of this action, the Japanese Ambassador called at the State Department to protest against the American curtailment of the export of aviation gasoline and scrap iron, and went so far as to declare that these restrictions might be considered as "an unfriendly act." Secretary Hull was extremely frank in his reply. He declared that it was really amazing for the Japanese government, "which had been violating in the most aggravating manner American rights and interests throughout most of China," to take such action. He inveighed against Japanese policy which appeared "bent on the conquest by force of all worth-while territory in the Pacific Ocean without limit as to extent in the south and in the southern continental areas of that part of the world." He asked how it could be expected that the United States should sit quiet and see most of Asia "Manchurianized," and declared that it was "unheard of for a country engaged in aggression and seizure of another country to turn to a third nation and seriously insist that the latter would be guilty of an unfriendly act if it did not cheerfully provide some of the necessary implements of war to aid the aggressor in carrying out its policy of invasion." He made clear the view of his government "that Germany and Japan were undertaking to subjugate both of their respective areas of the world and to place them on an international order and a social basis resembling that of eight centuries ago."

Language such as this makes it clear that by the fall of 1940 the American and Japanese governments had already arrived at a pretty complete diplomatic impasse in the Far East. For a period of nine years the United States had observed the onward march of Japanese militarism; it had seen Manchuria conquered; it had seen a large part of China overrun; it had seen the occupation of Northern Indo-China after the collapse of France; it had seen the power of the military clique grow by leaps and bounds; it now saw the authorities at Tokyo enter into a compact with the Axis powers to tie the hands of the American government, and at the same time protest against the exercise of the discretionary power which all governments possess to control the export of materials useful in the prosecution of war. The choice which confronted it as time went on was the choice between acquiescence in the triumph of a new policy of conquest, the abdication of American rights and interests in the Orient, the propitiation of the militarists in order to keep its hands free in the West, or the maintenance of its principles, and the giving of assistance to those who were contending for what it deemed to be its own interests and point of view in the Far East.

The alliance of September 27 had been countered by a new American loan to the government at Chungking. In December still further financial commitments were made, on the obvious theory that if the Japanese government had set out to tie the hands of the United States, retaliatory action was both proper and prudent. But beyond this the administration did not go; it was obliged by the circumstances of the time to move part of the fleet back into the Atlantic; and it willingly embarked upon protracted negotiations which were intended to immobilize and restrain Japan. On the other side of the Pacific, too, the militarists were not yet ready for the final test with the United States, and in March of 1941 there began the long diplomatic conversations with Admiral Nomura, the newly appointed Japanese Ambassador at Washington, which were only to be terminated with the attack upon Pearl Harbor.

So far as one may judge in the light of present knowledge, and of the documents published by the State Department, there was at no time any real meeting of minds between the two governments. There are hints in the correspondence already published that the Japanese would have been willing to "interpret" the treaty of September 27, 1940, in a sense favorable to the United States in exchange for a free hand in the Far East—in other words that they were ready to sell out their European allies if the price were right. But the fundamental question was that of China; and on this question the two governments were far apart at all times. In his proposals of May 12, 1941, Ambassador Nomura set no date for the removal of Japanese troops from China and he demanded that the United States abandon the régime at Chungking unless this latter consented to make peace with Tokyo.

In July there occurred events which indicated, even more clearly than any that had gone before, the limitless nature of Japanese ambition. The northern part of Indo-China had been occupied in July of 1940, which was bad enough; but on the twenty-second of July, 1941, under pressure from Berlin, the Vichy government granted Japan the right to maintain troops and air bases in Southern Indo-China. Such an agreement could only be construed as having the most aggressive implications; it clearly foreshadowed the attack on Malaya and Thailand which was to be unleashed at the end of the year. The American government acted promptly; on the twenty-third Acting Secretary of State Sumner Welles bluntly commented on these events to the Japanese Ambassador; on the twenty-fourth the President himself held forth to Nomura on the same subject; on the twenty-sixth an executive order froze all Japanese assets in the United States, with the consequence of virtually suspending all trade between the Island Empire and this country. In the days that followed, measures were taken to reinforce the American garrisons in the Philippines and the other American possessions in the Pacific; the clouds of war hung lower than ever. On the sixth of August the Japanese government responded to an American proposal for the neutralization of Indo-China with evasions, with the statement that it would withdraw its troops after the termination of the "China incident," on the condition that the United States would suspend all "military measures" and re-establish trade relations — in other words, it demanded little less than complete surrender.

Still the fateful moment had not come. There were, apparently, those at Tokyo who wished to delay — perhaps until the success of Hitler's campaign against Russia was a little more certain, perhaps in real dread of a clash with the United States. From Tokyo came a proposal for a personal meeting between President Roosevelt and the Japanese Premier, Prince Konoye; but there was little enthusiasm for this idea in Washington. On September 6 Ambassador Nomura submitted new proposals; but they were based once again on the Japanese having their way in China, did not even propose withdrawal from Indo-China, and again demanded cessation of military measures and resumption of normal trade relations. The tone had mounted, rather than otherwise; and the fact that it *had* mounted ought particularly to be borne in mind by those who cherish the romantic notion that severance of trade relations (such as had taken place in July) is an instrument of coercion preferable to and as efficacious as war.

The last act of the drama was enacted in November. The special mission of Saburo Kurusu to Washington needs no extended treatment here. In the nature of the case, it could be hardly more than a diplomatic ruse. It resulted in nothing more than a restatement of the issues between the two nations; an American proposal for a truce, based upon a relaxation of the freezing order on the one hand, and a Japanese commitment to stand still in Indo-China, died aborning. The news from the Far East steadily grew more menacing; the apprehensions of the State Department steadily mounted; and the last act in the diplomatic drama before Pearl Harbor was a personal appeal by the President to Emperor Hirohito, in which he urged His Majesty to withdraw his troops from Indo-China. The message was sent on December 6; on December 7, in an attack obviously planned long in advance, the Japanese assailed Pearl Harbor, and war was now begun.

The attack on Pearl Harbor was speedily described by the President in his address to Congress, requesting the declaration of a state of war, as "a date which will live in infamy." But its moral character is perhaps less important than its diplomatic consequences. Viewed from this angle, it accomplished what nothing else had done. It unified the American people; it opened the eyes of those who imagined that the United States could preserve peace without complacent acquiescence in aggression. And in the moment of crisis, Adolf Hitler and Benito Mussolini thoughtfully left no doubt of their own position. While the President and his advisers hesitated, perhaps with wisdom, the European Axis states declared war; the issue was posed in a fashion which terminated all debate; the unity which had been so difficult to arrive at had been forged by the act of the aggressors, as it was forged in 1917. A reluctant people had once more been driven into war; and with the sharp and inescapable challenge of December 7 the population of the United States girded themselves to meet their destiny.

By the comparative standard, it ought to be added, they were far better prepared than they had been twenty-four years before. The danger in which they stood had been more widely apprehended; and it had certainly been stressed, and vigorously, by the President of the United States. The navies which they needed to fight the war, though not yet adequate, had been immensely increased in the last years of peace, in 1938 to 1941 in particular, whereas the first great naval program in the earlier period had come only with the summer of 1916; the youth of the nation had been called to universal service nearly a year and a half before the struggle opened, whereas conscription came in 1917 only two months after our acceptance of the gage of battle; the industry of the nation had been more and more geared to war since the institution of the Office of Production Management in January 1941; the intensity of national feeling, as measured by the votes in Congress after Pearl Harbor, exceeded the feeling of the Wilsonian period. Not only the official view, but the view of many citizens affirmed the peril to be greater; the war of 1941 was not undertaken for the vindication of neutral rights, nor yet for the establishment of a lasting peace; it was a war of security, a war to protect the United States against the danger involved in the creation of two great military empires in Europe and in Asia. From the fall of France to the attack of December 7, this attitude had been steadily growing; neutrality had become a fiction long before it was abandoned entirely; and the events of 1939 to 1941 had demonstrated once again the truth that needs to be written firm and large on every American mind, *the truth that a great nation cannot isolate itself physically, morally, or intellectually from the rest of the world; that it cannot and will not suspend its judgments, or assume an attitude of cool detachment in the midst of world catastrophe; and that the only true prescription for "keeping the United States out of war" is the construction of an international order in which such conflicts as those of 1914 and 1939 do not occur at all.*

# VII

## War Diplomacy, 1941–1943

*The Second World War had seen the forging of a great alliance in the league of the United Nations. Especially notable is the close association of the major belligerents, an association much advanced by the declarations of Moscow, Cairo and Teheran. These declarations outline the future peace and the bases upon which it is to rest.*

### 1917 AND 1941

The circumstances of December 7, 1941, and those of April 6, 1917, invite comparison and contrast. After Pearl Harbor the United States found itself involved for the second time in a war of immense dimensions. For the second time it was called upon to bring its enormous physical power to bear on a gigantic scale. The task was obviously far greater than it had been twenty-five years before. In 1917 the struggle was confined to Europe, to all practical intents and purposes, and on the European continent itself the democratic forces had a bridgehead in unconquered and dauntless France. In 1941, on the other hand, the people of the United States were called upon to wage war on a truly global scale. They were obliged to carry on great operations in the Atlantic and Pacific alike. In the European war there was not a foot of soil, so far as the Continent was concerned, which could be utilized for the attack on their foe. In the Orient they were compelled to fight over distances the like of which had never been seen in war, and at an initial disadvantage that was tragically underlined by the Japanese conquest of the Philippines, their rapid advance down the Malayan Peninsula, the fall of Singapore, and the conquest of the islands of the Indies. A more colossal task has never been undertaken by any nation.

Yet the picture was not by any means wholly dark. For one thing, the relationship of the United States to the rest of the American republics was more solid and more cordial in 1941 than it had been at any time in our history. In the second and in part of the third decade of the twentieth century, the exercise by the United States of a police power over some of the Latin-American republics had been profoundly resented by the states of the New World. There was at times, perhaps, in the manners of certain American diplomats, and in the tone of public discussion, a superciliousness of attitude that did nothing to promote good relations. At the Pan-American Conferences of 1923 and 1928 the United States found itself the object of much suspicion, and even of positive hostility. But the turn of the tide was not long in coming. Already in 1927 the Morrow mission to Mexico, while by no means providing a long-range solution of the problems between the two countries, had set an example of the tone in which discussion ought to be conducted if we were desirous of winning the good will of our southern neighbors; the Hoover administration set itself in earnest the task of winning Latin-American esteem; under the leadership of Charles E. Hughes and Henry L. Stimson the way was prepared for the withdrawal of American troops from the soil of other American states, while a new interpretation of the Monroe Doctrine, which repudiated the notion of an international police power, did something to allay ill will. Still greater, however, were the achievements of the Roosevelt administration. Under the wise guidance of Cordell Hull, the United States in 1933 and still more unequivocally in 1936 accepted the doctrine of nonintervention in the affairs of independent states as a fundamental principle of action in the New World, and the protocols which established this principle were ratified with virtual unanimity by the Senate of the United States.

From this vantage ground the administration pressed on to the forging of closer bonds with the Latin-American republics. At the conference of Buenos Aires in 1936, a convention was adopted providing for mutual consultation in the event that the peace of the hemisphere was threatened; and in 1938 at the conference of Lima the means were found to provide a regular machinery for carrying out the obligation of 1936. In the latter conference, moreover, various measures were adopted against the threat of the totalitarian states; and the Declaration of Lima gave expression to the common ideals of the twenty-one states represented there. The outbreak of the European war drew closer these bonds; inevitably with the interruption of European trade the Latin-American republics turned to the United States for commercial and financial leadership as they had in 1914; and the constitution of a Financial and Economic Committee was the recognition of a practical necessity. At Havana in the summer of 1940, as has been already indicated, machinery was devised for the taking over of derelict territories in the New World, if such action should be necessary; and a declaration was signed stating that an attack on any one of the American nations should be considered as an attack on all. Common defense measures were established before our entrance into the war; the cordiality felt for the United States in Latin-American chancelleries had never been greater; and it received a striking testimony when, shortly after the outbreak of war, at the Conference of Rio, a resolution was adopted calling for a rupture of relations on the part of every American state.

Most of the states acted promptly; those in the Caribbean area in most instances declared war; and whereas in 1917 there were six states which held aloof from any demonstration of sympathy with the republic of the North, in 1942 there were only two, Chile and Argentina. Of these the latter had been persistently hostile to America, as she was governed by her Tory elements which feared the democractic impulses of the day, and which, in internal and in foreign affairs, were often in sympathy with the totalitarian states.

A second advantage in the diplomatic situation of 1941, as compared with 1917, lay in the greater solidity and power of Russia. When the United States entered the First World War, Russia was beginning that process of domestic change which was to culminate in the Bolshevik revolution and take her out of the war; but in 1941, on the other hand, as has been amply demonstrated by time, she was a powerful state, with resources immensely more developed, with a national will to victory that had been fortified by the deceptions of German policy and the brutality of German armed power. That she would contend with all her force against the invaders of her soil and the plunderers of her national domain was a conclusion almost inescapable; that she would engage vast armies, and inflict severe losses on the enemy, was equally clear. True, by a treaty which had been negotiated in April of 1941, and the value of which had been emphasized by a significant gesture of Stalin's, the Soviet Union was bound to observe neutrality in the Orient by a treaty of friendship with Japan; but, however distasteful this might be to the English-speaking nations from one point of view, from another it made it certain that the Russian armies would not have to fight on two fronts, and that they could devote the major part of their forces to resisting Germany. The significance of all this in the unfolding of events is evident enough today.

In still a third respect the United States enjoyed an advantage that it did not possess in 1917. It was much further advanced, as we have already seen, in its preparations for war than it had been twenty-four years before. It had enacted conscription nearly a year and one half before the beginning of war, instead of two months thereafter; its naval building program was a matter of years, not of months; its industrial production was already geared to war. These were real and substantial gains as compared with the situation in the First World War, and they provided reason for the belief that the United States would measure up to the great task to which it had set its hand.

Finally, the meeting of the President and Winston Churchill off the coast of Newfoundland in the preceding August had not been held merely for the purpose of drafting an ideal program, such as that laid down in the Atlantic Charter; the military and naval authorities of the two countries had consulted together exhaustively; and while their decisions were naturally locked in secrecy, it is not difficult to believe that the way had been paved for effective military and naval collaboration in the event of war. The total picture was not a bleak one, even though there were to be discouraging days ahead.

## The Declaration of the United Nations

Of the diplomacy of the period since December, 1941, it is far too early to write with authority. Yet certain large facts stand out, and these should be emphasized. One of the most important is the Declaration of Washington of January 1, 1942. Within a month after its entry into the war, the American government came forward with the text of a general agreement to be signed by all the nations at war. This agreement recognized the principles of the Atlantic Charter as binding; it pledged the signatories to an all-out effort and against a separate peace. It was so phrased as to permit the Soviet Union to continue its policy of neutrality in relation to Japan. But it was nonetheless far-reaching in its implications. It was signed by the United States, Great Britain, Russia, and China on January 1, and adhered to by twenty-two nations. Within the year it had also been adhered to by Mexico and by the Philippine Commonwealth. In contrast with the situation in 1917, the United States secured from its allies formal recognition of its proclaimed ideals at the very outset of the conflict.

There is one point about the declaration of January 1 that has received far less attention than it deserves. It was purely and simply an executive act. As such, what is its constitutional status? Is it within the competence of the President of the United States to bind the nation to make war in common with a large number of other nations, and not to make peace until these other nations make peace? An affirmative answer to this question might be given on the ground that to the President belongs the power of negotiation, and the power as Commander in Chief to carry on or to terminate hostilities. Yet the fact remains that so fateful a pledge has probably never before been made by the independent action of the Executive; and pondering upon it, and the almost general acquiescence in it, one wonders as to its long-range constitutional significance. The declaration of the United Nations constitutes a precedent which may be of very great interest for the future.

## Relations with Latin America

In the forging of the common bonds that ought to unite the nations at war against the Axis, American diplomacy has in many respects been extremely successful since the outbreak of the war. In the course of the year 1942 the two neutral nations in the New World were reduced to one. In Chile, where an election had taken place in February, 1942, a rising popular clamor demanded a severance of relations with the Axis; in October Acting Secretary of State Sumner Welles, after consulting with the other American belligerents, made an important speech denouncing the South American neutrals as providing important centers of information and bases for espionage to the Nazis and their friends; at first the Chilean government's reaction was one of annoyance, and a visit of President Rios to the United States was canceled; but shortly thereafter the government at Santiago sent one of the most important of the members of the cabinet, Señor Morales, the Minister of the Interior, to study the situation at first hand, and after his return, on January 20, 1943, relations were broken with the Axis.

There were other important events in the field of Latin-American relations, and in reference to the war, in 1942 and 1943. In July, Mexico declared war on the totalitarian states, following the torpedoing without warning of several of her vessels in the Gulf of Mexico. The friendship newly sealed between the United States and its southern neighbor was further emphasized when in the spring of 1943 President Roosevelt entered Mexico and met President Avila Camacho at Monterrey. An ambitious program of economic collaboration followed hard upon this historic meeting. In August of 1942, Brazil entered the war against Germany and Italy. In September an agreement was announced with Ecuador, by which the United States was permitted to establish bases on the Galápagos Islands, and on the western tip of the Ecuadorian coast, at Santa Elena, thus affording new protection to the area of the Canal. The solidarity of the American states was further attested when the Inter-American Emergency Advisory Committee for the Political Defense of the Western Hemisphere gave pitiless publicity to memoranda prepared in the United States which revealed the widespread activity of

Axis agents in the Argentine. In the spring of 1943, indeed, a military *coup d'état* in Argentina awakened hopes that the last of the Latin-American republics would come to the side of the Allies. At long last, indeed, the new government did break with the Axis. But it remained authoritarian in its viewpoint, and it sought to stir up trouble in Bolivia and Paraguay. Nonetheless, taking the picture as a whole, in the winter of 1944, the unity of the American nations was substantial, and the resources of the Americas had been mobilized to a degree that was by no means possible in 1917.

## Relations with Britain and Russia

The fundamental question, however, was the relationship of the three great powers engaged in the war against Germany. With Britain, of course, there was already an intimate understanding before the United States entered the conflict. The meeting of the President and the British Prime Minister in the summer of 1941 had underlined that understanding. The actual participation of the American government in the conflict gave it added strength and purpose. Never, perhaps, in the history of international intercourse have two great nations achieved so high a degree of collaboration. The meetings of Mr. Roosevelt and Mr. Churchill became a regular part of the conduct of the war, and these meetings, important as they were in the political field, were supplemented by exchanges of views between the military and naval authorities which not only evolved a common policy, but resulted in such an intermingling of British and American forces and commands as is almost without precedent. There were jealous voices raised from time to time as to the terms and character of this intimate co-operation. But they affected little the actual course of events, or the temper of American public opinion. It was indeed remarkable when in the summer of 1943, from the platform of the oldest of American universities, Winston Churchill proclaimed his desire for a continuing close association between Great Britain and the United States. It was still more remarkable when the Governor of the State of New York, an ambitious and realistic politician, echoed this desire. True, there were voices raised in dissent from such a proposition, and with some reason, if such an association was to be regarded as exclusive, or limited in its terms. But there were few who doubted that Anglo-American understanding was desirable, and the course of time affirmed rather than controverted the movement towards intimacy and close accord.

The forging of close relations with the Soviet Union, however, by no means advanced so rapidly. The background of Russo-American intercourse was, of course, far less favorable to such relations than in the case of Great Britain. The American government did not even recognize the government at Moscow till 1933, being one of the last great states in the world to do so. Nor was this recognition the prelude to a period of unalloyed good will. The hopes of increased commercial intercourse that had been raised with recognition were not fulfilled. The pledges that were made by the Kremlin were not always adhered to. The Russian policy of appeasement in 1939, the Russian attack on Finland (so it was viewed in the United States), were hardly likely to improve the diplomatic atmosphere. Finally, the State Department went so far as to administer a sharp rebuke to the Soviet Union at the time of the Russian occupation of the Baltic republics — that is, in the early summer of 1940. Naturally, this rebuke was not well received at Moscow. The expression of unqualified moral judgments, either official or unofficial, rarely adds to the ease of international intercourse, and is, perhaps, a habit to which Americans are too much given. After all, the Russians had their own philosophy to justify the methods and objectives of their diplomacy, and could hardly be expected to enjoy being lectured from the other side of the Atlantic. Relations between the U.S.S.R. and the United States were by no means cordial at the end of the year 1940, and American diplomacy faced an important, indeed an essential, task in working to improve them.

A change for the better occurred at the very beginning of 1941, some months before Hitler's momentous decision to invade the Soviet Union. The State Department received word of the Nazi leader's design, and communicated this news to the Russian Ambassador in Washington. It repeated its warning in the spring. The actual outbreak of war was followed by the immediate despatch of a mission to Moscow, and, as we have already seen, Averell Harriman followed promptly on the heels of Harry Hopkins. Aid to Russia was forthcoming in large quantities, and in June of 1942 a master-plan of lend-lease was drawn up, which was effectively administered in practice.

American diplomacy played a part, also, in the epoch-making Anglo-Russian agreement of the twenty-sixth of May, 1942. By this remarkable compact, Great Britain and the Soviet Union agreed to collaborate with each other as well as with the other United Nations in the peace settlement and in the ensuing period of reconstruction. They bound themselves to enter into no negotiations with the Nazis or any other government in Germany that "does not clearly renounce all aggressive intentions." They agreed to act together "to preserve peace and resist aggression in the post-war period." They laid down as a principle of action the general proposition that "they seek no territorial aggrandizement for themselves," and that they intend to pursue a policy of "non-interference in the affairs of other nations." There seems to be little question that in all this the two nations concerned had the blessing of the

United States, and that the terms of the Anglo-Soviet pact are in part a restatement of the Atlantic Charter and the Declaration of Washington.

Nor were all the signs of good will confined to the spring of 1942. In November, in an important speech, Marshal Stalin defined the issues of the war as "the abolition of racial exclusiveness, equality of nations and integrity of their territory, liberation of enslaved nations and restoration of their sovereign rights, the right of every nation to arrange its affairs as it wishes, economic aid to nations that have suffered and assistance to them, in attaining their material welfare, restoration of democratic liberties, destruction of the Hitlerite régime." In the spring of 1943, in a gesture that was widely applauded at the time, the Third International was disbanded; the natural assumption from such a step was that the Kremlin was seeking good relations with Great Britain and the United States.

Still there were difficulties in the relations of Moscow with the Western powers. The Russians, encouraged by the Presidential declaration of May, 1942, as to the "urgent need" of creating a second front, were undeniably much disappointed by the limited scope of Anglo-American operations in the months that followed. There was an acid touch in Stalin's famous interview with an American newspaper correspondent in October, in which he declared that all that was necessary was for the democracies to "fulfill their engagements on time." The operations begun in Africa in November of 1942, however brilliant they may have appeared to American and British opinion, were not regarded as meeting the necessities of the case in Moscow. In the summer and early fall of 1943 Russian newspapers, which, while they did not necessarily represent the government, could not, of course, speak without its consent, were still dwelling on the relatively insignificant military contribution of the Western powers, in a fashion that suggested irritation and resentment. It was clear that there existed an opinion in Russia that the Union of Soviet Republics was being made to bear more than its fair share of the burden of war; after all, Russian sacrifices were enormously greater than those of the United States and Great Britain; and the splendid victories of the Russian armies could hardly fail to accentuate the conviction at Moscow that the major credit for the destruction of Hitlerism must be given to the armies of Marshal Stalin.

Politically, too, there were signs of unresolved differences, if not of actual conflict. It was made clear again and again by the government of Marshal Stalin that the Baltic regions must be regarded as a special interest of Moscow, and that the western frontier of the Soviet state would remain where it had been set in the summer of 1940; it was by no means clear that this view of the matter had been accepted at Washington. It was also made clear that the proposal for a confederation of states in Eastern Europe, a proposal that had some support from Mr. Churchill in a radio speech of March, 1943, was by no means acceptable to Russia, that it suggested to Russian minds a design to insulate the rest of Europe from the Communist heresy. There seemed to be a difference of opinion between the Soviet government on the one hand, and the British and American on the other, as to the two rival anti-Axis factions, the "partisans" and the supporters of General Mikhailovitch in Yugoslavia; the rift between Russia and the Polish government-in-exile in the spring of 1943, not yet healed at the end of the year, could not fail to embarrass the relations of the Western powers with Moscow. The absence of Russia from the conferences at Casablanca, at Washington, and at Quebec, could be explained by those of optimistic temperament (as it was by Prime Minister Churchill) as due to nothing more than Stalin's reluctance to trouble his relations with Japan, with whom Russia was at peace, and by the Russian leader's preoccupation with the military campaign; but less cheerful commentators persisted in representing it as the sign of something less than complete cordiality and of a genuine difference of political views. The existence of Polish refugees at Moscow, who constituted a "committee" under the control of the Russian Foreign Office, the similar existence of a German committee which prepared in the summer of 1943 a ringing manifesto to the German people to shake off their oppressors, the recall of Litvinov from Washington and of Maisky from London (both these men being known as the friends of co-operative action with the democracies), suggested to some observers that a political understanding with the Soviet Union had not been arrived at and was badly needed. There was much talk of a tripartite conference as autumn came on; there were even important conversations in London between Sir Anthony Eden, the British Foreign Secretary, and the Russian Ambassador, who returned for a little to London with the avowed purpose of promoting an accord, but no one could yet say whether such an accord was feasible, or whether the autocrat of the Kremlin could be brought to discuss the questions of Europe in a diplomatic conference in which he might find himself opposed by such a formidable combination as President Roosevelt and Prime Minister Winston Churchill.

There was also a question, and a highly important one, as to whether the three states saw eye to eye as to the conditions under which the war might be ended. At Casablanca in January, 1943, the President and the Prime Minister had proclaimed the objective of the war as the "unconditional surrender" of the enemy, and this phrase remained unqualified and almost unconstrued until the late summer of the same year. It was not at all sure that a similar theory was held in Moscow. In one of his rare speeches Stalin had hinted that the overthrow of Nazidom was the main objective of the Soviet Union, and that Russia had no interest in the extinguishing of German military power; and the emphasis which he laid on the expulsion of the enemy from the territories of the great Slav state suggested to some minds that were this end achieved Russian enthusiasm for the complete military destruction of Germany might slacken substantially.

Such were some of the difficulties emphasized by the pessimists in the early fall of 1943. But these difficulties proved to be superficial, and the forces that made for understanding to be dominant. As the year lengthened, the possibility of a three-power conference at Moscow broadened into a certainty; the very fact that it could be held was a favorable sign, and men had a right, therefore, to await with expectation the results of the momentous meeting between the Foreign Ministers of the three nations which opened on the nineteenth of October. By this time the Russians had immensely improved their military situation; the Germans had been driven back from the valley of the Don not only to the Dnieper, but beyond; the fate of the Nazi forces in the Crimea was almost sealed; and the victories of Marshal Stalin's armies had been made easier, it could hardly be denied, by the great achievements of the Western powers. For in November of 1942, a landing of British and American forces had been effected in North Africa, and in the months that followed General Montgomery's gallant Eighth Army, advancing from Egypt, and the British and American forces under General Eisenhower, moving eastward into Tunis, had beaten the Nazis decisively, and freed the whole of the African continent from the grip of the Axis powers. Even more, they had, in a brief campaign of thirty-eight days, overrun and conquered Sicily, an event which was accompanied by the fall of Mussolini and the collapse of the Fascist régime; they had landed on the heel of the Italian boot, and fought their way northward beyond Naples; they were engaging important forces which barred the way to Rome. At the same time, throughout the spring and summer of 1943, American and British bombers ranged day and night over Germany; by the end of October (it was claimed) they had destroyed no less than 1,000,000 lives, and rendered more than 7,000,000 people homeless; they had reduced German productive capacity by at least 20 per cent, and wreaked incalculable destruction in seventeen of Germany's fifty most important centers of production. And added to all this, a steady flow of American and British materials of war had poured in upon the Russians, making a signal contribution to the striking power of Stalin's armies. It was evident that the immense resources of the English-speaking peoples were more and more being brought to bear upon the guilty architects of the Second World War; and it is more than probable that all these facts had weight in the formation of the attitude of the government in the Kremlin.

At any rate, whatever the processes of thought that went on in the mind of the leader of the Russian people, the results of the Moscow conference surpassed all expectations. In almost every field of endeavor they marked a tremendous step forward. In a joint Four-Nation Declaration, to which China was admitted along with the three Western powers, future policy was laid down in its broad lines. The preamble of this declaration expressly declared that the "unconditional surrender" of the Axis powers should be regarded as the basis of common action by the Allies. The declaration itself provided (1) that this common action should be continued after the end of the war "for the maintenance of peace and security" (2) that the signatory powers "recognize the necessity of establishing at the earliest practicable date a general international organization, based upon the sovereign equality of all peace-loving States, and open to membership by all such States, large and small, for the maintenance of peace and security"; (3) that pending the realization of this purpose the signatories would consult with one another "with a view to joint action on behalf of the community of nations"; (4) that after the termination of hostilities they would not "employ their military forces within the territories of other states except for the purpose envisaged in this declaration, and after joint consultation"; (5) that they would seek to "bring about a practicable general agreement with respect to the regulation of armaments in the post-war period."

In addition to these general declarations, at least one specific question was treated at Moscow in definite and unmistakable terms. The three Foreign Ministers declared that they wished "to see re-established a free and independent Austria," "liberated from German domination." This statement was an important one. It meant, clearly enough, that Germany was to be shorn of the annexations which Hitler had carried through; it suggested a territorial settlement at least as drastic as Versailles. Had the authors of the Moscow pronouncement on Austria been charged with violating the principle of self-determination by their action, they would doubtless have answered that it was by no means certain that in 1938 Austria had wished to be annexed to the Reich. They might have gone further. They might have argued that an independent Austria had been proved necessary to the very existence of Czechoslovakia; for Hitler, once he had taken possession of the Austrian lands, had been in a position to outflank the Czech military line. At any rate, whatever the reasons for their action, Hull and Eden and Molotov had given warning that the peace of the future was not likely to be tender of German feelings; they had, by this first statement with regard to territory, underlined the doctrine of unconditional surrender which had been once more stated at Moscow.

The conference at Moscow naturally gave rise to a wave of optimism as to the future of Russo-Anglo-American relations. The events that followed before the end of the year tended to confirm this optimism. For, with the ground thus prepared, it was possible to arrange for a meeting of the chiefs of state, or rather for two such meetings, and in the month of December there took place the conference of Cairo and the conference of Teheran. The first of these dealt chiefly with the affairs of the Orient, and was participated in by President Roosevelt, Winston Churchill, and General Chiang Kai-shek. Its purely Oriental aspects ought not to be considered at this point, since we are here considering the drawing together of Russia and the Western powers. But it was significant that at Cairo the regaining of Manchuria by China was put forward as one of the objectives of the war in the East. Such a declaration, it was widely assumed, could not have been made without the tacit consent of Moscow, especially since it immediately preceded the meeting of the British and American leaders with Stalin; and it tended, therefore, to refute the cynicism of those who had been predicting that Russia had her own very definite Manchurian ambitions.

The climax in the crescendo of Russian relations with Great Britain and the United States came, of course, at Teheran. There the three great leaders met in intimate and personal conference, in an atmosphere of great cordiality; there they reiterated the purposes that had been declared at Moscow; and the end of 1943 registered the greatest advance yet made toward genuine unity of purpose in the waging of the war. With 1944 we approach the contemporary scene; and with Teheran we may end the historical summary of our war diplomacy in the West, so far as it deals with the problem of Russo-American relations.

## Relations with France

A word needs to be said, however, with regard to American relations with France, and with regard to the problems created by the occupation of Italy. The value of the policy of maintaining relations with Vichy during 1941–1942 should be clear to every thoughtful man. For some time the drift of the Pétain régime toward Hitler was arrested, the French fleet and the French colonies kept out of the hands of the Germans. As late as February, 1942, when Weygand, the French commander in Africa and a known enemy of the Nazis, had been dismissed by the aged Marshal, and the role of Admiral Darlan had become greater and greater, a renewed pledge was asked of and given by the Vichy government with regard to both the position of the French navy and the French North African empire. In the meantime, through our observers in North Africa, the way was prepared for the invasion of the latter part of the year. Judged purely by its results, in the saving of American lives, in the preparation for the brilliant campaign of 1943, there can be little question of the wisdom of the course pursued by the governments of the United States and Great Britain.

But the invasion itself created a new situation, and presented some difficult problems. Naturally, it led to the rupture of relations with Vichy; but, by the merest chance, Pétain's henchman, Admiral Darlan, was in Africa at the moment when our troops landed, and for a time he was recognized by our military commander as the authorized ruler of the North African colonies. The reasons for this were, of course, purely practical; Darlan seemed to be in a position to command the loyalty of the French commanders on the spot; he was able to put an end to hostilities very shortly after they had begun; and he thus provided a protection for our armies which enabled them to press on rapidly with their task. At the same time the deal with Darlan was profoundly distasteful to many Americans; and it was naturally even more so to the Free French in London, and to their leader, General Charles De Gaulle. There were the makings here of a very pretty tangle, and one which might have the unhappiest consequences for the future. The situation was not altered when, at the end of December, Darlan was assassinated; the government at Washington now desired to sponsor the leadership of General Giraud, whose romantic escape from Germany, whose gallantry and disinterestedness, made him in many ways an appealing figure. But Giraud was without political interests or distinguished political capacity; and it was doubtful whether his influence with Frenchmen could ever be that of the gallant leader who, in the dark days of 1940, had refused to admit defeat. To leave him in complete control in North Africa did not seem to fit the situation.

The State Department yielded slowly and somewhat reluctantly to these incontrovertible facts. It had been annoyed, just after the entry of the United States into the war, by a sort of Free French *coup d'état* on the islands of Saint Pierre and Miquelon, off the coast of Newfoundland, which had up to that time been held by a Pétainist governor. There were signs, too, that De Gaulle represented a kind of militant French nationalism that might be difficult to deal with; and the personal qualities of the General, despite his undoubted courage and patriotism, were not altogether ingratiating. It may be that British pressure was applied, and applied quite vigorously, before a solution was worked out. But the solution came, nonetheless. A French National Committee was constituted at Algiers, and was recognized as "administering those overseas territories which acknowledge its authority" subject to the military requirements of the Allied command. This committee did not operate without friction, and it sought not unnaturally to enlarge its role; its political leadership came more and more into the hands of De Gaulle, but all in all, despite heartburnings and controversy, it appeared as if the way were being found to admit France once more to a place in the councils of the nations. That this was desirable, even necessary, there were few disposed to deny.

## Italy and Its Problem

The invasion of Italy presented another sort of problem. The doctrine of "unconditional surrender" proclaimed by Roosevelt and Churchill was here applied for the first time. On the twenty-fifth of July, the conquest of Sicily having been completed, the tottering Fascist régime came to an end; Mussolini was ousted from power by a vote of the Fascist Grand Council itself; and King Victor Emmanuel called Marshal Badoglio to take charge of the badly leaking Italian ship of state. For a time the new régime may have been deluded enough to believe that it would be permitted to relapse into neutrality if they would go through the motions of renouncing or abolishing Fascism; but such an assumption was, of course, ridiculous. Neutrality for Italy would have balked the democratic nations of the fruits of their victory; it was obviously not to be considered. Nor were the British and Americans disposed to bargain; they demanded and received capitulation. This capitulation was followed by the surrender of the greater part of the Italian fleet, by the cessation of all hostile effort, by Italian co-operation against the Germans, and even by co-belligerency. While, in view of German violence and power, it did not result in the easy occupation of the whole peninsula, it certainly operated to advance substantially American military interests and to accelerate the military progress of the democratic nations.

In the meantime, an effort was made to illustrate in practice how benevolent, mild, and constructive an Allied occupation might be. The establishment of the Allied Military Government in Sicily was accompanied by the repeal of the laws against the Jews, by the grant of a new freedom to the press, by the establishment of a judicial procedure which protected the rights of the citizen; measures of economic assistance were speedily put on foot; and while out-and-out Fascists were deprived of their posts, there was no such political proscription of local functionaries as would have seriously disorganized the life of the island. It is still too early to judge the effects of this procedure; and it would not be strange if some American critics should object that too much that existed was left standing. But to this it might readily be answered that it was not the intention of the democratic nations to determine for the Italians what, at the end of the war, it was hoped they might determine for themselves; and that, in the circumstances of a military occupation, it was hardly wise to throw too heavy a burden upon the occupying forces, or undertake a complete renovation of Sicilian political institutions. AMG in Sicily and, later, in Southern Italy, was only a first step; its establishment opened up a long vista of complicated problems with which the future would have to deal.

At the same time the policy of "unconditional surrender," as applied in Italy, was by the end of the year clearly revealed as implying an opportunity for the Italians to return to democratic institutions. One of the results of the conference at Moscow, in fact, was a declaration (a declaration, be it emphasized, in which the Russians joined) by which it was indicated that the objectives of Allied policy would be the strengthening of the forces of popular rule, and the recognition at the end of the war of the right of the Italian people to choose their own form of government. This declaration was important. It not only clearly defined a policy for this beaten nation, but suggested that possibly a similar principle would be applied to the Germany that would emerge from the ruin of Hitlerism.

## Relief and Rehabilitation

One other important decision was made in 1943, big with significance for the future. It was sometimes contended that the doctrine of unconditional surrender was unduly harsh, that it left to the vanquished no hope for the future, and thus prolonged the war. The argument was balanced by many very important considerations, and by the experience of 1918; but President Roosevelt gave a partial answer to it in August when he declared that unconditional surrender did not mean that the people of the Axis nations must "trade Axis despotism for ruin under the United Nations" and added that the aim of the latter was to permit "liberated peoples to create a free political life of their own choosing, and to attain economic security." This statement was supplemented by action. In November 1943 was created the United Nations Relief and Rehabilitation Administration, participated in by almost all the nations at war. The general framework of this agency of peace and reconstruction had been determined before the end of the year, and the omens were favorable for obtaining for it the necessary financial support. Here at least were a promise and a hope of constructive and generous action in healing the wounds of postwar Europe, and of practical and far-reaching co-operation on the part of the great coalition engaged in war against the enemies of mankind.

## American Diplomacy and the Orient

Of the diplomacy of the United States with regard to the Orient, it is necessary to speak only with the utmost brevity. In the early stages of the war, the Chinese, and the Australians too for that matter, were by no means satisfied with the strategy which seemed to give, and did indeed give, the major weight to the operations in Europe; and numerous and eloquent were the appeals for greater aid. But as the war in the East proceeded more prosperously, as the Americans made good their footing on Guadalcanal, and with their allies drove back the Japanese on New Guinea, the clamor died down. The events of 1943, moreover, tended to tranquillize the Chinese, whose government, beset by the most difficult military and economic problems, sorely needed encouragement. The association of China with the three great Western powers in the declaration of Moscow was important. But still more important, of course, was the declaration of Cairo. In this great statement of war aims, the doctrine of unconditional surrender was stated as flatly for the East as it had already been stated for the West; Japan, it was declared, was to be expelled from all the "territories she had taken by violence and greed," from the islands of the Pacific, from Malaya and Burma and Siam; Korea was to become independent; not only Manchuria, but also Formosa and the Pescadores were to be restored to China; and thus a strong and powerful bulwark was to be erected against Japanese ambition in the future. The significance of this program was all the greater, since it came just before the conference of Teheran; the silence in Moscow suggested, though it did not prove, that the Russians were not unfavorable to the conclusions that had been reached. All in all, then, the picture of United Nations diplomacy in the Orient seemed to have been somewhat clarified by the end of 1943; and though there was little doubt that the declaration of Cairo committed the British and American governments to "serious and prolonged operations," to use the language of the declaration itself, there was no reason to believe that it did not meet with the approval of British and American opinion.

## Postwar Plans

There was one other point of interest in the purposefully vague and general definition of war aims by the democratic nations. There was no definite policy and no understanding with regard to the revival of the League of Nations. Perhaps there was not complete agreement on this point. In an obviously inspired article (one that deserved much attention for the picture that it gave of Mr. Roosevelt's viewpoint as of April 10, 1943), Mr. Forrest Davis seemed to indicate that the President was far from favorable to the revival of the League, or at any rate to the revival of the issue of American adhesion. One can understand this point of view. On the far less important question of American ratification of the World Court protocol, the administration had sustained one of the most resounding of its defeats. The vote of 1935 on this question was not of happy augury as to what the Senate might do to an attempt to revive the issue of American approval of the Covenant. The whole matter was such as could be easily bedeviled by unscrupulous politicians; and there were all too many people who had not forgotten the passions, and the partisanship, of 1919 and 1920. Furthermore, there was something to be said for the view that the institutions of peace ought to be permitted to develop by a kind of gradual and inevitable process, rather than be created out of hand. This has been the way, in no small degree, with the growth of Pan-American relations; the development of the United Nations Relief and Rehabilitation Administration suggested that it might conceivably be the way with the association of the United States with Europe. There would be a vast number of tasks to be undertaken in common at the end of the war; might it be that, in the doing of them, international agencies would develop, so to speak, spontaneously, and be all the more solid because they grew out of actual need and practical necessity?

On the other hand, it was by no means certain that what seemed to be the American point of view on this matter would meet with the approval of the nations of the Old World. Mr. Churchill, in one of the most interesting and forward-looking of his speeches, seemed to think somewhat differently; the League, after all, despite its complete failure to prevent a new and general war, was a going institution in many respects; it had attracted to itself loyalties and attachments; some of its organs, for example the International Labor Office, though transported from Geneva, were still in existence. One of its outstanding strengths during its twenty-odd years of activity was that it provided a forum in which the small and less important states could express their point of view on international affairs; it was possible that these same states, on this very ground, would wish to see it revived. But no definite steps had been taken in this direction by the beginning of 1944.

In the meantime, the disintegration of Hitler's Europe proceeded. Nowhere were the Nazis able to win the affections of those whom they coerced or persuaded into sharing their fortunes. Signs multiplied that the allies of 1941, Hungary, Bulgaria, Rumania, were sick to death of their bargain. Guerrilla warfare flared up in Greece, in Yugoslavia. The French people stirred uneasily beneath the weight of their chains. The Norwegians persisted in their sullen resistance. Belgians and Dutchmen awaited with eagerness the day of liberation. Even the Danes, treated relatively kindly by Nazi standards, revolted against the odious domination of Berlin. In every theater of the war, indeed, the omens were favorable; and by the end of 1943 the question of the hour was not, Who would win the war? but, How durable would be the peace?

### Summary

*How shall we sum up the diplomacy of the war years that we have traversed? In the first place, we may say that the most powerful coalition in history had been constructed to resist the ambitious disturbers of the peace. This coalition had grown stronger, not weaker with time; its core was the three great nations, Russia, Great Britain, and the United States, in the West, and again three great nations, China, Great Britain, and the United States, in the East. In both areas of activity much progress had been made in the definition of common aims; in the West not only had plans been laid, albeit indefinite ones, for a new organization of "peace-loving" nations, but the three great powers had pledged themselves to stand together to impose disarmament upon Germany and to maintain peace and security; and they had begun to sketch in the terms of a new territorial settlement, a settlement which implied that Hitlerite Germany was to be stripped of its spoils. In the East, also, much ground had been cleared: territorial objectives had been clearly defined, at least to a substantial degree; the pattern of the future, in the event of a United Nations victory, was becoming visible. Great indeed were the sacrifices ahead; but diplomacy had done a large part of its work, and much, perhaps most, of what remained depended upon the valor of the soldiers and sailors of the contestants, and upon the resolute will and unbreakable purpose of the people of Britain and the United States.*

# VIII

## The Past, Its Lessons, and the Future

*The past proclaims that "isolationism" is outworn gospel. Peace depends upon (1) the effective disarmament of Germany and Japan, (2) the harmonious co-operation of the victor nations, (3) the evolution of international institutions for the better solution of the broad economic and political problems of the international society. It depends too upon the sagacity of the American people, their choice of leaders, and the working of their constitutional mechanism. Finally, it is related to the success of our own domestic economic order.*

### Isolation Impossible

We have now reviewed the course of American foreign policy from the year 1898 to the moment at which we stand. Such a review ought to be something more than an academic exercise. For the first time in our history as a nation, men of middle age today have seen two world wars in their own brief lifetimes. They have been, or at any rate they ought to be, the beneficiaries of that experience. They have a chance to apply the lessons of the past—of their own past—to the future that lies ahead. What have they learned? What ought they to learn from the history of the last thirty years?

*They have learned, first of all, or at any rate should have learned, that to imagine that the United States can remain aloof from a major European struggle is to imagine a vain thing.*

In the World War of 1914, in the World War of 1939, impartial judgment was, from the first, impossible. Americans made up their minds about the merits of each of these struggles almost as soon as the guns began to roar. They were simply incapable of saying, "It doesn't matter," or "One side is just as right as the other." Even those who called themselves isolationists, or who wished to keep out of the struggle, rarely were willing to do this. Rightly or wrongly, Americans in both wars insisted upon making moral judgments, and when they had made them they were influenced by them. They could not help being. Of course the nation was not unanimous in 1914; it was not unanimous in 1939. But there was a strong desire to see one side win and the other side lose; and this desire was bound to influence policy.

Starting with this initial prejudice, in the war of 1914 the government of the United States adopted a policy, a policy more favorable to Great Britain than to Germany. It took a stand as early as February, 1915, which meant war if the Germans persisted in sinking merchant vessels without warning. After the destruction of the *Lusitania,* retreat from this stand was virtually impossible. For a time we were able to avoid war, first by the diplomacy of delay, and second by the temporary abandonment by Germany of the U-boat warfare. But when the challenge was again offered in 1917, there seemed to most Americans only one course open — to fight. It was Woodrow Wilson, of course, who made up and shaped the issue. But at every critical moment, so far as we can measure the matter, he was sustained by American public opinion. Not he, but the American people, chose the course that led to war.

It was much the same in 1941. From the outset of the World War in 1939 the American people had their partialities. In the case of Europe there was from the beginning a desire to express this partiality in action, as indicated by the repeal of the embargo on munitions in the very autumn in which the war broke out. But the fall of France intensified this feeling. A fear of consequences was added to a moral repugnance to the Nazi régime. We thus made up our minds to assist Great Britain; the lend-lease enactment was the result. Lend-lease implied more than at first appeared; it soon involved the patrolling of the Atlantic, a challenge to the U-boat. The old issue was shaping up when we were relieved of the necessity of a decision by the German and Italian declarations of war on the United States.

In the years 1939–1941 our spokesman was Franklin D. Roosevelt. But Mr. Roosevelt no more determined policy by his arbitrary will, or in a vacuum, than Woodrow Wilson had in 1914–1917. Isolationism, in the sense of complete abdication of moral judgment, in the sense of complete submission to German ambition, was not in accord with American opinion. And war came.

These two experiences ought to make every American reflect. Is it likely that we would act differently if, after an interval, Germany once more challenged the peace of the world? Is it not clear that unless we wish to be involved in a third holocaust, Europe must be organized for peace? How can one avoid this conclusion?

Nor can we hope to remain aloof from the affairs of the Orient, either. Such action is possible theoretically, no doubt, but the history of the last forty years suggests that it is not possible practically. We made commitments in the Far East as early as 1898. There have been times when we did not wish to use our power there, but there has been almost no time when we were willing to pay the price of isolationism, in the form of abstinence from moral judgment and complete noninterference in Asiatic questions.

We intend to restore the independence of the Philippines. Shall we leave them unprotected against a revival of Japanese power? We have done much to encourage the growth of a strong China. Are we going to cease to be interested in her development as soon as the war ends? It is difficult to believe so.

*The answer, then, to the deep-seated yearning for peace which is found in most Americans does not lie in withdrawing behind a frontier that, in the present kind of world, may hardly be said to exist. It lies in a sincere effort to find a positive program based on experience and adequate to maintain tranquillity for a long time to come. Such a program must be a matter of general principles, not of infinite details. The details must grow out of the principles. They must be worked out in a complex and ever-changing world, not today or tomorrow, but over a long generation. But they must be part of a broad policy, and that policy is not difficult to state. It consists in some simple essentials:* (1) *the effective disarmament for a long period to come of Germany and of Japan, as the disturbers of the peace in our own time.* (2) *As both a condition of this disarmament and an essential of peace in and of itself, the harmonious cooperation of the victor nations.* (3) *The evolution of institutions for the better solution of the broad economic and political problems of the international society. Each one of these points requires elaboration, and to that we now turn.*

## The Disarmament of Germany and of Japan

The tragedy of the war in which we are engaged lies in the fact that it might easily have been prevented, had we been just a little wiser. It was we, we and our European associates, who permitted Germany to grow strong again after less than twenty years and challenge the peace of mankind. Hitler came into power in 1933. He soon began to step up the rearmament of

Germany. The United States, Great Britain, France, all stood by and watched the process, while the Fuehrer became more and more arrogant, flouted the processes of peaceful adjustment, and issued one challenge after another to the rest of Europe. United pressure in 1933 or 1934 could have prevented German rearmament. Prompt action against the German occupation of the Rhineland in 1936 could have made war practically impossible. The construction of the vast military machine that now terrorizes Europe could have been prevented. Shall we let it, at the end of this war, be reconstructed once more?

With the technical problem as to what are the best measures to insure the effective disarmament of Germany this book is not concerned. The purpose here is to emphasize the general principle, and to warn against the error that permitted us to apply imperfectly and then to abandon that principle after the last war.

The trouble was that we began to feel sorry for the Germans and to question the "justice" of the Treaty of Versailles. Our failure to prevent the military recovery of the Reich was tied up with our conviction that our former enemies had much to complain of. How shall we avoid making a similar mistake again?

We should, of course, aim at a peace that does not shock the moral sense of moderate-minded men. We must not dismember Germany; we must not pursue any kind of policy so ruthless as to provoke a reaction of sympathy later; we must not deny to the German people a chance to better their economic condition in the future. We are committed to an independent Austria; we are likely to see the Sudetenland restored to the reborn Czechoslovak state; we may see other territorial changes that will not be palatable to Hitler and his friends. So far as possible, when new frontiers are drawn there should be some chance for the transfer of populations on both sides of the line, with a view to creating a stable situation. I have already mentioned the excellent precedent of the Greco-Turkish settlement of 1921; perhaps there will be room for the application of a similar method after the present war. If it *does* prove practicable, it will be a great factor in bringing about more stable conditions in the future.

*But whatever territorial settlements are made, one thing we must remember. We cannot permit Germany to rearm on the plea that it does not like those settlements. We have seen what this means already. A rearmed Germany would not stop with the rectification of "injustice." It would go on once more, as it has in the last decade, to challenge the tranquillity of all Europe. There is no reason why we should have any doubts on this point.*

In the Orient, the same general considerations apply. There again history tells us the same story. Great Britain and the United States permitted Japanese militarism to grow to its present dimensions. The Washington treaties amounted to the renunciation of force by this country in the Far Pacific. The policy of 1931, willing to wound and yet afraid to strike, accomplished nothing. The power of the militarists increased. To that increase we opposed moral homilies and mild forms of economic pressure. We met the issue squarely only when we were forced to do so by the action of Tojo and his underlings, and met it a decade too late. The British were no less blind than we.

To have made this error once was excusable enough. But we certainly ought to have learned our lesson by now. We certainly ought to be resolute in keeping Japan disarmed for a long time to come, and we must not let some kind of false sentiment blind us to this necessity.

As a matter of fact, we are less likely to be deceived into

relaxing our vigilance in the Orient than in the Occident. Traditionally, action has been a little easier for us there. Moreover, the territorial settlements are not likely to be quite so complex. The terms already laid down as those to be imposed on Japan seem to most Americans "just." There is little reason to believe that that view will change very quickly.

And yet there have always been apologists for Japan on the ground that she needs room for her surplus population, and more markets for her products. Such apologists have rarely weighed these considerations against many others, against Chinese population problems and hopes of future development, against the threat to Filipino independence offered by Japanese expansion, against the suffering that a ruthless and unchecked militarism can inflict on others, against the corrosive and far-reaching effects of violence in international affairs. We ought not, after this war, to deny to the Japanese, any more than to the Germans, the hope of economic recovery. But neither ought we to be gulled into permitting them to arm once more before another generation has come to manhood. And we must be ready to apply force to *prevent* that rearming; we must not wait until the military machine has again been perfected and is ready to challenge the peace of a large part of the world.

## The Unity of the Allies

So much, then, for the first of our three propositions as to the bases of peace. The second is the unity of the Grand Alliance itself, of the three great military nations now in arms against Germany—that is, of Russia, Great Britain, and the United States. It is obvious that this unity is essential to world peace from two all-important points of view. First, to maintain the disarmament of Germany and of Japan. Should the Grand Alliance be ruptured, should Russia be alienated from her present allies, or Britain from the United States, our enemies would pluck up heart, would intrigue to gain for themselves a free hand, would be able to reconstitute their power. Second, the danger might then present itself of a war between the present allies, a war which might be more dreadful and more prolonged than that in which we now find ourselves. The unity of the three great military powers of today is a prime necessity of a peaceful future. We need, therefore, to examine some of the conditions of happy relations in the future with London and with Moscow. Not that the preservation of these relations lies entirely in our hands. It lies in part with the peoples of Great Britain and Russia. But there must exist in this country the resolution to do our part, an understanding of the nature of the problem, a sense of its difficulties, and a determination to surmount them.

## THE UNITED STATES AND BRITAIN

*There are many reasons why the interests of the United States and Britain run parallel, and why, therefore, their diplomacy should remain united. They are both "satisfied" powers, which desire tranquillity in the world at large, and have no ambitious designs of conquest to satisfy. They would both be menaced, as they have been menaced in the past few years, by the growth of a strong European power which controlled the air or the sea routes across the Atlantic. In the Orient they both desire a field for the profitable investment of their capital, and a chance to compete freely and fairly for the markets — as they hope, expanding markets — of that part of the world. Security in the East as in the West is for them a matter of vital significance.*

There exists, moreover, a habit of accommodation between them. For a period of a century and a quarter, they have settled every difference that has arisen between them without resort to war. Their relations have been extraordinarily harmonious, on the whole, since 1898. The British indeed have almost made it a rule of policy to avoid a quarrel with the United States. They will probably continue to do so, and from the angle of British interests there could be nothing more desirable than to secure the backing of this country for a long era of peace and tranquillity. Never, moreover, have relations been better than they are today. The intimacy of Roosevelt and Churchill, the frequent conferences between them that dramatize and therefore heighten the sense of common purpose, the extraordinary military and naval collaboration that has brought the armed forces of the two nations to operate in great degree in concert, all these are hopeful indications for the future.

On the part of Americans, if the existing harmony is to be preserved, it is important to keep several things in mind. *In the first place, let us not be shallow enough to imagine that because it is to Britain's interest to court the United States, it is not to our interest to co-operate with Britain in the maintenance of world tranquillity.* The costs and the sacrifices of the present war ought to disabuse us of any such fundamental error. The avoidance of the repetition of the present struggle is and ought to be one of the principal objectives of American diplomacy. We shall not achieve this end, as the past has demonstrated, by refusing to assume responsibility. We shall not achieve it by walking alone. We need Britain, as Britain needs us.

*In the second place, Americans need to remember that they are not the custodians of the British Empire, or of the regions committed to Britain's charge.* We may have our own ideas as to how Britain should deal with the question of India, or the question of Palestine, or the question of Egypt. But we can hardly expect to be successful in directing the solution of these questions, any more than we should expect the British to tell us what to do about Puerto Rico, or Samoa, or the island bases that we may maintain in the Pacific at the end of this war. There is far too much sentimental and ill-informed discussion of many British problems in the American press and in the American Congress. There exists among too many Americans the belief that such problems can be solved by catchwords, such as "independence" or "democracy." The *direction* of British rule, as the direction of our own, has usually been towards a wider measure of freedom and popular government for the peoples in its charge. But the timing of such measures, the reconciliation of them with order and genuine economic progress, is a matter on which few Americans are entitled to speak with authority. We should, for the most part, not try to do so.

It is not unlikely, however, that some of the difficult problems with regard to territories that come into the possession of the Allies as a result of the war can be solved by Anglo-American agreement on the basis of the principle that was put forward twenty-four years ago at Versailles. The idea of the mandate, of the administration of backward regions under international supervision and control, is an idea that has much merit. It may prove useful and practicable in the future. Let us bear it in mind when we come to discuss these matters.

*In the third place, let us beware of those elements in our own country who, for one reason or another, seek always to widen the distance between the two peoples.* It is not difficult to understand the age-old prejudices which animate some of our population where Britain is concerned. It is more difficult to be charitable with regard to those newspapers which play upon these prejudices, and inflate them by sheer misrepresentation. But however we may judge anti-British sentiment, let us not be swayed by it into the rupture of the happy relations which now exist. No doubt, in the postwar period, there will be many differences between the two nations, questions of trade, of tariffs, of airways, of bases, of naval power. But there is not one of them that cannot be reasonably settled if the American people wish it so. We must not let any specific controversy cause us to lose sight of the fundamental community of view which ought to unite American and British policy.

## The United States, Russia, and World Peace

Our relations with Russia constitute a more difficult problem. Though not by any means untroubled (there have been unpleasant episodes since Teheran) they have certainly improved since the summer of 1942. The resolution of the United States to fight the war through, the mounting scale of assistance to the U.S.S.R., the victorious campaigns in Africa and Sicily, were bound to produce their effect. The meetings of the Foreign Ministers in Moscow, and of the great war leaders themselves at Teheran, were skillfully used to bring about the maximum degree of understanding between Russia and the Western powers. It was wise and forward-looking policy to invite Russia to a place on the Mediterranean commission, and to set up a new European commission in London on which the Russians would be represented. On the other side, the suppression of the Third International, the dying down of the clamor for a second front (a clamor which could not have arisen without the tacit consent of the Kremlin), the tone and temper of Stalin at Teheran, all give reason to hope that the desire for understanding is mutual. Russia, like the United States, is a great, one may fairly say a satiated, nation. Russian interests, like American, truly considered, will best be served by a long period of peace and reconstruction. Russia, like this country, ought to fear a revival of German, or indeed of

Japanese, militarism. There is no reason why the countries should not pursue the same objectives, or why they need to clash with each other.

Yet it would be an undue optimism that saw no dangers ahead. *One of these dangers lies in the territorial questions in which Russia is specifically interested.* The Russians have made it clear beyond question that they wish for the most part to retain the frontiers which they established in 1939 and 1940; that is, that they wish to keep control of the region which once constituted the Baltic states of Estonia, Latvia and Lithuania, and of most of that part of Poland which they overran in 1939. With regard to the first of these claims, Russians point out that historically the Baltic provinces had long been Russian down to 1919, that they enjoyed only a brief independence from 1919 to 1939, that they had moved away from democracy towards Fascist or semi-Fascist régimes (Lithuania in 1926, Latvia and Estonia in 1934), that there are sound strategic reasons for Russian possession of this territory, and that *before* Russia subscribed to the Atlantic Charter the inhabitants thereof declared by their own popular vote for union with the U.S.S.R. On the other hand, many inhabitants of these little states, and of course their ministers in Washington (who still remain at their posts), denounce Russian action as a violation of that same Atlantic Charter, demand the right of self-determination, and condemn the popular votes held under Soviet auspices as meaningless and fraudulent. In the question of Eastern Poland, there is the same sort of difficulty. Russians would doubtless claim that the majority of the persons living in the territory taken from the Polish Republic were Russian by blood and sympathy, and that they wished to remain within the boundaries of the great Soviet fatherland. They have suggested that Poland compensate herself in East Prussia for her losses to the eastward. The Poles, on the other hand, at the time that this is written still deny the rightfulness of the Russian claim to the territory taken in 1939, and have so far refused to be appeased by a territorial bargain farther west.

It is not necessary to express a final judgment on these questions. Perhaps (though it is very doubtful) the Russians will retreat from the position which they have taken. Perhaps we may be able to persuade them to some kind of compromise which is acceptable to all concerned. But if they do not, what then? *There are Americans who would rather not deal with Russia at all unless they could deal with a Russia which in every respect accepts American notions of international justice and right. There are Americans (and it is a melancholy thing to say it) who, for partisan ends, or to promote the isolationism in which they believe, are ready to inflate these territorial questions into an issue which will produce a rupture, or at least a coldness, in Russo-American relations. There is here one of the great dangers of the future.*

*But there are other than territorial questions which may divide Russia and the United States. The difference in the institutions of these two states is very great.* Fanatical Communists on the one hand, fanatical defenders of the American *status quo* on the other, can do infinite harm in the future. The danger, of course, has been much reduced by the Russian suppression of the Third International. But it has not been completely dispelled. We need to adopt towards Russia's internal order a balanced and fair-minded attitude. There are many reasons for believing that it could not possibly operate in such a country as our own, with its strong dislike of government authority, our highly developed capitalism, our national instinct for adjustment and compromise rather than sweeping economic change. But for the Russians, the Soviet system works, and is carrying the country triumphantly through a bloody and costly war. Why should we seek to impose our standards upon others any more than we would wish them to impose their standards on us? Why should we permit differences of economic organization to create a rift between us?

The same principle applies in the political field. The notions of freedom so dear to the Anglo-Saxon have no application in the land of the Soviets. Perhaps they will grow there. But we must avoid the peremptory or the evangelizing tone in dealing with the Kremlin. We must not raise issues of principle to the point of irritating and alienating those who might be our friends. We have gotten along again and again with Latin-American states which are less than loyal to our own democratic conceptions. We are at this moment allied with a Brazil which is governed by a dictatorship. We could not, without embarrassment, investigate the political principles of some other of the so-called republics of the New World. Why start a quarrel over doctrines with the nation with which it is to our highest interest to maintain good relations?

There is another matter about which we should be thinking if we desire good relations with Russia. The Russians have suffered as we shall never suffer in the present war. Their devastated villages and countryside, their broken homes, their crippled industrial machine, the base brutality and ruthlessness of German military methods, all these things will make our Soviet allies extremely harsh when it comes to dealing with the Reich. Even under different and more favorable circumstances, the Russian standards of humanity would not be those of the United States. We must be prepared for acts that will not be at all lovely, and which we ourselves might not commit. We shall have to judge them with some measure of charity, while striving to point out the dangers of a severity so great as to lead to a reaction in favor of the vanquished.

There may be other possibilities of controversy as the future unfolds. It is too much to hope that there will not be. To solve them wisely we must keep steadily in view the large objective, the supreme interest in unity. Our attitude towards the U.S.S.R. is a matter of resolute determination to retain the friendship which we are gaining in war. If we do not let ourselves be misled by a perverted idealism, or bedeviled by the agitation of mischief-makers, we ought to be able to preserve that friendship for a long time to come.

## China

In the case of the Orient, the unity of Russia, Great Britain, and the United States ought to be supplemented by close relations with the new China. It is obvious that in the East this great, populous and gallant nation may well serve as a guardian of the peace against a reborn militarist Japan. It is obvious, also, that for this country good relations with the Chinese present no very special difficulty. The tradition of friendliness is strong. The interests of the two countries may well be complementary. We may hope to play a part in Chinese economic development; without our capital and that of Great Britain it would be difficult for the vast resources of China to be mobilized for the benefit of the Chinese people and of the world. We cannot, of course, predict with confidence what the future of this great nation will be. It is by no means certain that all our hopes with regard to it will be realized. But we know enough to be sure that it is wise statesmanship to encourage the growth of a strong state in the Far East, and we may be reasonably sure that the American people will be favorably disposed towards such a course of action.

## International Institutions

If we have once laid broad and deep the foundations of unity amongst those great powers whose collective force is indispensable to the peace of the world, *then, and only then,* can we hope for the development of effective international institutions on a grander scale. Such institutions can perform a great variety of useful tasks, both in the political and in the economic sphere. There is room, for example, for the judicial settlement of many of the minor disputes arising between nations; the revival of the World Court, and American adhesion to it, is a reasonable objective for the future. The general international conference assembling at regular intervals, and represented by the meeting of the League Assembly in the twenties and thirties, may play a useful role in international politics, and might conceivably be revived. On many economic problems, the consultations of the great powers need to be and ought to be supplemented by the opinions of the less powerful states.

There are, however, two ways to go about constituting these institutions. One way is to draw up elaborate and ambitious blueprints, covering a great variety of possible situations. The other is to let these institutions evolve out of the needs of the international society as those needs are made clear. There is, in my judgment, a great deal to be said for the second way. This is the manner in which the fabric of Pan-Americanism has been wrought and made useful to larger and larger tasks. It is the manner in which we have already begun to deal with postwar problems, through such agencies as the International Food Conference held at Hot Springs in May of 1943, and the setting up of the United Nations Relief and Rehabilitation Administration. If we proceed along this path, we may find a place for those League agencies that have survived the storm of war; we may even find room for the association of the smaller states with the larger in the work of maintaining peace and ensuring the continued disarmament of Germany and Japan; but we shall avoid the dangers, the difficulties and the contentious debates which attended the submission of the

Covenant of the League of Nations to the Senate in 1919 and 1920. We shall run less risk of disillusionment for the future if we proceed step by step than if we set up an ambitious and all-comprehensive scheme which becomes the target for all kinds of criticism, and every detail of which tempts to debate and controversy.

## The Politics of the Matter

Such is the general outline of the policies that may bring peace to the world in the future. To carry them out is, however, less easy than to formulate them. The success of such policies depends in part upon the political sagacity of the American people, and upon the adaptation of the American constitutional mechanism to the task; and it depends, too, upon economic circumstance, and the manner in which the complex economic problems of the postwar era are faced. Let us look at these two matters for a little. And let us again refer to history, and to the events of 1919 and 1920.

One reason for our failure then lay in the fact that our proper role in international affairs became the subject of a partisan debate, and that this debate reached its climax in a Presidential year. Had President Wilson accepted the Senate reservations in the fall of 1919, this result might have been avoided. Instead, he chose deliberately to inject the issue into the campaign of 1920. Nothing could have been more dangerous. About the last place to look for fair-minded, temperate discussion is in the midst of a Presidential campaign. About the last person to whom to look for absolutely frank, clear expression of opinion on a great public question is a Presidential candidate. Woodrow Wilson could not prevent his Republican opponents from adopting a platform that was intended to attract both the friends and the foes of the League. He could not prevent the Republican candidate from making speeches which sometimes squinted at acceptance, and sometimes suggested repudiation, of the Treaty of Versailles. He could not prevent the exaggerations, misrepresentation, and widespread appeals to national selfishness, the most shortsighted selfishness, that are the easy devices of politicians in the search for votes. By throwing the matter into the elections, he confused and blurred instead of clarifying the issue. But he did more than this. He hazarded the success of his own cause. For when the Republicans won a tremendous victory, it was easy to represent this victory as a repudiation of everything that the Democratic administration had stood for. The country had been fatigued, not enlightened. No doubt many persons had voted for Harding in the hope that he would lead the way to the ratification of the Covenant. But, in the ranks of the victorious party, the real resolution and determination lay with the irreconcilables. They knew what they wanted and were prepared to fight for it. The League supporters were timid, and tired. They acquiesced almost without a fight in the policy of a separate peace with Germany, a policy that was the repudiation of everything for which Woodrow Wilson had contended.

The lesson of 1920 is one that can and ought to be learned by those who conduct the foreign policy of the United States, or by those who play a leading role in its political affairs. There seems evidence that it has been learned by the present Chief Executive. Mr. Roosevelt has borne himself very differently from Woodrow Wilson. He has not appropriated to himself the great ideal of international organization in the almost apostolic fashion of his predecessor. He has let public sentiment express itself, rather than prodding it into action. His adhesion to the great declaration of Moscow came only after the House of Representatives, by a decisive vote, had committed itself to the general principle of an international organization, and just when the Senate was preparing to act in similar fashion. He has not offered a provocative or partisan word on this weighty subject. Nor has his Secretary of State. Few men are more intense or more tenacious in their convictions than Cordell Hull. But few men have been willing to practise more forbearance in the fulfillment of their purposes, and few have commanded a wider confidence on both sides of the aisle in the Senate Chamber on Capitol Hill.

Nor has the opposition party set out, as did Lodge and his followers, deliberately and in some instances maliciously, to block the administration as it has moved forward along the path of international organization. Ex-Governor Landon, it is true, has struck the note of suspicion. But ex-Governor Landon has never been an imposing figure. It is more significant that last September the bigwigs of the Republican Party at the Mackinac conference committed themselves to a forward-looking view on international questions; that Wendell Willkie has lent the force of his personality and the weight of his name to the same cause; that Senators like Burton of Ohio and Ball of Minnesota have contended manfully in the Senate for an affirmative policy in international affairs. Certainly there has not yet developed the bitter and dangerous partisan rift on questions of foreign policy that was so disastrous twenty-four years ago.

It is not probable, of course, that the question of international organization in any concrete form will be ready for discussion this year. We should certainly be excessively cheerful to imagine that in the course of the next few months we would both finish the war and draft the peace. If we accomplish the first, we ought not to hurry about the second. There is no reason, therefore, to fear that we are on the verge of another such partisan brawl as that of 1919 and 1920.

Yet it is a melancholy fact that the foreign policies of the

United States have more than once been bedeviled by partisan politics. It is a melancholy fact that in choosing their national leadership the American people have all too often been indifferent to the importance of international affairs. It is useless to imagine that we can make headway in these great matters if the electorate is to be swayed by every unscrupulous appeal to selfishness and passion, or if it cannot and will not distinguish between the statesman with a broad view of the future and the politician who has nothing to contribute but platitudes and cautious nothings. The personality of the President of the United States, or of any President of the United States, cannot be regarded as of no importance in dealing with the vast problems ahead. We must have men in the White House who believe in the great objectives we have been discussing, and who have the courage and the political genius to translate them into action.

## Peace and Our Government Machinery

There is no reason to be pessimistic about the operation of our constitutional mechanism. There are many persons, it is true, who blame the events of 1919 and 1920 on the constitutional requirement of a two-thirds vote in the Senate for the ratification of treaties. Certainly this requirement complicated the problem, as it did later the far less important question of American adhesion to the World Court. But there have been remarkable developments since the First World War. They are not wholly new, but they have attained a new importance. We have, in the recent evolution of our foreign policy, found ways to avoid the embarrassments connected with the two-thirds rule. There are several such ways. One is by acts of legislation, which take the place of treaties. The Hull reciprocity agreements, no less than twenty-five in number, by January 1, 1943, were all negotiated under the authority of an act of Congress, and required no special approval by the Senate. In the same way the lend-lease policy, involving as fundamental a decision as was ever made in the field of foreign affairs, was framed not in the form of a treaty, but in the form of national legislation. A recent agreement with Panama, which aroused considerable opposition in the upper house, was carried out in the same fashion. The method that has been applied in these cases can be applied in others.

There is another expedient which equally commands attention. The President possesses large powers to negotiate, without Senate action. Thus, at the end of the Spanish-American War, President McKinley fixed many of the conditions of peace (the disposition of the Philippines excepted) by the protocol which he signed as Commander in Chief of the Army and Navy. The armistice agreement of November 11, 1918, determined in some measure the bases of the Treaty of Versailles, since both victors and vanquished accepted the Fourteen Points as the basis of action. When our enemies lay down their arms in this war, the terms of the armistice may give the answer to many problems. Some, indeed, like the territorial settlements to be made in the Far East, have already been fixed by the Declaration of Cairo. That declaration is likely to be honored.

Interesting too, and hopeful, is the growth of an international procedure which encourages agreement by means less formal than treaties. The Pan-American Conferences, for example, frequently adopt resolutions which have binding force, but which are never submitted to any legislative body for ratification. More recently, the United Nations Relief and Rehabilitation Commission was set up without any formal diplomatic understanding—and yet there it is today.

It is not necessary to be alarmed at any of these procedures. Almost any important diplomatic policy sooner or later demands some kind of legislation, and usually some vote of funds. We do not need to worry about the danger that these new procedures will tend toward undue executive power. On the contrary, they represent a practical means of dealing with important problems on a truly democratic basis, and yet bar obstruction such as has sometimes proved so annoying in the past. They deserve to be encouraged, not condemned. They *will* be encouraged, if the American people really wish to pursue the great objective of helping to organize the world for peace.

## Peace and Economics

There is a final aspect of the vast problem of international peace that cannot be escaped. One of the reasons for the breakdown of the system of Versailles lay in the Great Depression. The humors of a diseased economic policy communicated themselves to the body politic. The peace-loving nations were, in the decade of the thirties, too busy with their own problems to deal effectively with those of the international community.

We shall face the most complicated economic problems that we have ever faced at the end of this war, both in the national and in the international field. We shall, it is to be hoped, not repeat the ridiculous experiment of attempting to collect reparations or war debts across national frontiers, while at the same time we exclude, by high tariffs, the goods by which alone war debts and reparations can be paid. We should either frankly wipe the slate clean or pursue such fiscal policies as make repayment possible. We shall not, it is to be hoped, reduce Germany and Japan to a dull despair, and by so doing encourage a reaction of sympathy in their favor that might have consequences as fatal as did the revulsion of feeling in favor of Germany after the last war.

We shall have to deal boldly and successfully with our domestic problems. If we do not find a way to conduct our own affairs more wisely than we did in the twenties, if we embark upon domestic policies that lead to inflation and from inflation to violent reaction, if we have to deal with vast numbers of unemployed, and with severe social tensions, the chances are that we shall not act wisely in the international field. The internal problems ahead of us will be many; their solution will not be easy; but they must be faced constructively, with hope and courage. Here, as in other matters, the errors of the past may help to illuminate the future.

## Summary

As we contemplate and analyze the difficulties of the post-war era, there is no room either for inconsequent optimism or for cynicism and despair. It is in the nature of man, or at any rate of many men, to demand a final solution of the vast problems of humanity. In a period of war, of the most extensive and colossal of all wars, it is natural that men should begin to yearn for peace, and should try to find it in some quick and easy way. History offers little hope that it can be secured without steady effort and unquenchable resolution. The problems of mankind are continuous. In facing these problems, we should be instructed by the past. *Here in America we may be taught by it that we cannot, if we will, dissociate ourselves from the problems of the international society, that we must face realistically the fact that force is an element in the triumph of what we deem to be not only to our interest, but in the interest of our own ideas of justice and right, and that we must be prepared to exercise it in concert with like-minded nations. We must not be misled into abdicating the place of influence and power to which the war has brought us. For America has shown that it cannot be content with what has historically been described as "isolationism," and the question of the future is not whether we will or will not play a great role, but whether we will play such a role consistently, worthily, and in the interests of all mankind.*

# Index


ADAMS, HENRY, 7
Alaskan boundary dispute, 24
Albania, 121
Algeciras, Act of, 19
*Algonquin*, S.S., 50
Allied Military Government, 177
Alsace-Lorraine, 60, 70, 87
Alverstone, Lord, 24
Angell, Norman, 18
Anglo-Japanese alliance, 24–25
Anglo-Russian agreement, 166–167
Archangel, 90, 92
Argentina, 65, 66, 160, 164
Armament, reduction of German, 84–85; postwar reduction of naval, 112–113
Armenia, 8
Armistice negotiations, First World War, 70–78
Atlantic Charter, 145–147
Austria, 117, 172; German, 76, 87–88; Germany occupies, 106
Austria-Hungary, 17
Avila Camacho, Manuel, 163

BADOGLIO, MARSHAL, 176
Baker, Ray Stannard, 98
Baldwin, Stanley, 16, 105
Balkan Wars, 17, 19
Ball, Joseph H., 201
Beck, James M., 57
Bernstorff, Count von, 49
Bethmann-Hollweg, 49
Blaine, James G., 7
Bliss, General, 73
Bolivia, 65
Bolsheviks, 67, 92
Borah, Senator, 122
Bosnia, 17
Boxer revolt, 28
Brazil, 65, 163, 196
Brest-Litovsk, Treaty of, 67, 90
Bruening, Chancellor, 104
Bryan, William Jennings, 12, 20, 25, 37, 41, 63
Bulgaria, 69
Bullitt mission, 92
Burgess, John W., 7
Burian, Count, 69
Burton, Harold H., 201

CAIRO, Conference and Declaration of, 173, 179–180, 203
Canada, 4
Caporetto, 67
Caribbean Sea, 4
Caroline Islands, 27, 96
Carranza, General Venustiano, 66
Casablanca, conference at, 168, 169
Central America, 65
Chamberlain, Joseph, 22
Chamberlain, Neville, 134
Charles, Emperor, 69
Château-Thierry, 69
Chile, 65, 66, 160, 162–163
China, 63, 64, 113; Open Door Policy in, 13–14; American policy toward, 96–97; Ameri-

can loans to, 123, 152; American relations with, 197
Churchill, Winston, 91, 125, 134, 165
Clayton-Bulwer Treaty, 23
Clemenceau, Georges, 84, 95
Cleveland, Grover, 6, 7–8
Colombia, 65, 66
Communism, 105
Constantinople, 61
Continentalism, 3–4; United States forsakes, 5–9, 11, 30
Cordial Understanding, France and Great Britain, 16–17
Covenant, League of Nations, 80–84
Cuba, 4, 8, 9, 10, 65
Czechoslovakia, 85, 88, 103, 106

Danish West Indies. *See* Virgin Islands
Danzig, 87
Darlan, Admiral, 143, 144, 174–175
Davis, Forrest, 180
Dawes Plan, 116
Declaration of London, 39
Delcassé, M., 19
Denikin, General, 91
Depression of 1929, 103, 116, 117–118, 204
Dewey, Admiral George, 10, 26
Diederichs, Admiral, 26
Diplomacy, American, in First World War, 46–52, 53–62; postwar, 107–116
Dominican Republic, 65, 66
Dumba, Dr., 45

Ecuador, 65, 163
Eden, Sir Anthony, 169
Eliot, Charles William, 34
Espérey, General Franchet d', 69
Estonia, 194
Ethiopia, 83
Expansion, United States territorial, 4, 12; German ambitions for, 28

Finland, 165
Fiske, John, 7
Fiume, 102
Florida, purchase of, 4
Foch, Marshal, 68, 73
Foreign policy, development of American, 11–13, 14, 16, 19, 20, 30; German, 29; American postwar, 107–111
Foreign trade, American, 4; German competition in, 28
Four-Nation Declaration, Moscow, 171–173
Four-Power Pact, 124
Fourteen Points, 60–62, 71, 73, 75–76
France, postwar, 105–106; American relations with, 174–176
Francis Ferdinand, Archduke, 17
French National Committee, 176

Galápagos Islands, 163
Gaulle, Charles De, 175, 176
Gerard, James W., 44
Germany, 17; naval expansion, 16; American relations with, 26–30, 127–128, 147–150; democratic government in, 75; postwar, 84–85, 103–107; disarmament of, essential, 186–188
Giraud, General, 175

Gold standard, United States departs from, 118
Grand Alliance, disintegration of, 101–107; unity of, a necessity, 189–190
Great Britain, American relations with, 20–26, 46–48, 123–126, 130, 164–165, 190–193; reverts to policy of balance, 102–103, 104–106
*Great Illusion* (Angell), 18
Greco-Turkish agreement, 86, 117
Greenland, 142
Grey, Sir Edward, 39, 54
Guam, 113
*Gulflight,* S.S., 42

Haiti, 65, 66
Harding, Warren G., 110–111
Hare-Hawes-Cutting Bill, 114
Harriman, Averell, 166
Hawaii, 5–6, 8, 16
Hawley-Smoot tariff bill, 118, 125
Hay, John, 13
Hay-Pauncefote Treaty, 23, 25
Henry, Prince, 29
Henry-Haye, Gaston, 144
Hertling, Chancellor von, 69
Herzegovina, 17
Hindenburg, President von, 69, 70, 104
Hindenburg Line, 69
Hitler, Adolf, 74, 75, 88–89, 122, 127, 186–187; rise of, 104, 105, 106, 115
Hoar, George Frisbie, 11
Hopkins, Harry, 145, 166
House, Colonel E. M., 20, 36–37, 48, 54, 55, 68, 75
Huerta, General, 25
Hughes, Charles Evans, 116, 158
Hull, Cordell, 144, 151, 158, 201
Hull reciprocity treaties, 118, 119, 126, 202
Hungary, 117

Iceland, 142
Indo-China, Japanese occupy, 151, 153, 154, 155
Inter-Allied Conference, Paris, 68
Inter-American Emergency Advisory Committee, 163
Inter-American Financial and Advisory Committee, 137
International Food Conference, 198
International institutions, a requisite for the future, 197–199
International Labor Office, 181
Interventionists, 11
*Intimate Papers* (House), 20
Iraq, 144
Ireland, British repression of, 108
Irish Free State, establishment of, 124
Irish Home Rule Bill, 26
Isolationism, American, 3–4, 110; the retreat from, 5–9, 11, 30, 119–123, 126, 128–129, 139; impossible in light of past events, 183–186
Italian-Tripolitan War, 19
Italy, 17, 61, 67, 83; after Treaty of Versailles, 102, 105; invasion of, 176–178

Japan, 63, 90, 119, 120; Pacific colonies of, 95–98; growing

postwar tension with, 128, 130; militarist power in, 137–138; crisis with, 150–155; disarmament of, essential, 188–189
Jellicoe, Lord, 51

Kaiserism, 57–58
*Kearny,* U.S.S., 149
Kellogg Pact, 111
Kiaochow, 63, 64, 96
Kolchak, Admiral, 91, 92
Konoye, Prince, 138, 154
Kurusu, Saburo, 154

Landon, ex-Governor, 201
Lansing, Robert, 37, 39, 41, 44
Lansing-Ishii memorandum, 97
Latin America, American diplomacy in, 64–66, 158–159, 162–164, 196; United States seeks to strengthen position in, 137
Latvia, 194
Laval, Pierre, 143
League to Enforce Peace, 54, 55, 59
League of Nations, Wilson propounds, 54–55, 59; weakness of, 80–84; other aspects of, 98–100; America defeats, 107–111; the question of revival, 180–181
Leahy, Admiral, mission to Vichy, 143–144
Lend-Lease policy, 134–142, 203
Liliuokalani, Queen, 5–6
Lima, Declaration of, 159
Lippmann, Walter, 57, 128
Lithuania, 194
Little Entente, 103
Lloyd George, David, 84, 87, 95
Lodge, Henry Cabot, 7, 12, 201
London Economic Conference, 118, 125, 126
London, Treaty of, 62, 102
Louisiana Purchase, 4
Ludendorff, General, 69, 70
*Lusitania,* S.S., 31, 42–43, 44

McKinley, William, 5, 9, 10, 203
McLemore, Jeff, 44, 45
Mahan, Alfred Thayer, 7, 15
Manchukuo, Japanese establish, 114
Manchuria, 63; Japanese occupy, 113–114
Manila, battle of, 10
Marshall Islands, 96
Matsuoka, Yosuke, 138
Max, Prince, 70–74 *passim*
*Memoirs* (Lansing), 37
Messersmith, George S., 104
Mexico, 65, 66, 158, 162, 163
Mikhailovitch, General, 168
Minorities, national, 86–87
Monroe Doctrine, 8, 23
Morocco, 16, 17, 18–19, 29
Moscow Conference, 170, 171–173
Munich Conference, 106, 120
Murphy, Robert, 143
Mussolini, Benito, 171, 176

National Socialism, 51; German, 75, 78
Naval expansion, United States, 14–16; German, 16
Navy League, 15
Neutrality, American, in First World War, 31, 34–35, 37–46, 51–52
Neutrality Acts, American, 115–116, 120, 121

Neutrality Board, American, 41, 47
Neutrality Proclamation, Washington's, 35
*New York World,* 45
Nine-Power Treaty, 113
Nomura, Admiral, 152, 153, 154
North Africa, invasion of, 170, 174–176

Office of Production Management, 156
Olney, Richard, 21
Open Door Policy, 13–14, 24, 64
Orient, American diplomacy in, 62–64, 137–138, 179–180
Ottawa Imperial Conference, 1932, 125
Ottoman Empire, 62
Oumansky, Constantine, 145

Page, Walter Hines, 38
Panama, 65, 66, 203; Canal, 23, 25
Pan-American Conferences, 66, 137, 203
Pan-Americanism, 198
Paraguay, 65
Peace, aspects of international, 202–206
Pearl Harbor, Japanese attack, 155–156
Pershing, General J. J., 73
Peru, 65
Pétain, Marshal, 143, 144
*Philip Dru, Administrator* (House), 37
Philippines, 27, 113, 162; United States acquires, 10–13; movement for self-government, 114–115
Poland, 85, 87, 103, 105, 123, 194
Prague, 121
Princip, Gabrio, 17
Propaganda, British, in First World War, 33
Puerto Rico, 4, 10

Rehabilitation, 178
Reparations, First World War, 76, 93–95
Reparations Commission, 116
Republicans, 8
*Reuben James,* U.S.S., 150
Rhineland, 84, 87, 105
Robins, Raymond, 67
Roosevelt, Franklin D., 200; endeavors to maintain peace, 119, 120–123; policy of, prior to collapse of France, 132–136; and passage of Lend-Lease Bill, 139–142; changes neutrality legislation, 149–150
Roosevelt, Theodore, 7, 9, 15, 18, 28, 34, 57, 66
Ruhr, 116
Rumania, 61, 85, 103
Russia, 59, 60, 61, 67; and Versailles settlement, 89–92; isolation of, 102; American diplomatic relations with, 144–145, 165–174, 193–197; in Second World War, 160
Russo-German treaty, 106, 107
Russo-Japanese War, 29, 63

Saar, 87
Salisbury, Lord, 7, 16
Salvador, El, 65
Samoa, 5, 6, 16
Sarajevo, 17
Security, Wilson and national, 55–57
Selective Service Law, 136

Self-determination, national, in Europe, 85–89
Serbia, 85
Shantung, 63, 76, 96–97, 113
Siberia, 90–91, 92
Sicily, 176, 177
Sims, Admiral, 19
Smuts, General Jan, 93
Soissons, 69
Spanish-American War, 4, 9–13, 22
Spanish Civil War, 105
Spring-Rice, Cecil, 36, 38, 55
Stalin, Joseph, 167, 170
Stimson, Henry L., 114, 158
Strong, Josiah, 7
Submarine warfare, First World War, 31–32, 34, 39–45, 46–51 *passim,* 53, 66–67, 71
Sudeten question, 76, 88, 106, 120
Supreme War Council, 68
*Sussex,* S.S., 46

Taft, William Howard, 19, 54
Tariff legislation, American postwar, 117, 118
Teheran, conference of, 173–174
Territorial settlement, question of, in First World War, 58–61
Third International, 167, 193, 195
Thrasher, 41
Transylvania, 61
Treaties, secret, in First World War, 61–62, 64
Triple Entente, 17
Trotsky, Leon, 67
Turkey, 69
Twenty-one Demands, 63–64

United Nations Relief and Rehabilitation Administration, 178, 198, 203
Uruguay, 65

Vandenberg resolution, 123
Venezuela, 65; boundary dispute, 7–8, 21; England and Germany blockade, 23, 27
Versailles, Treaty of, and League of Nations, 79–84; disarmament of Germany under, 84–85; territorial settlements under, 85–89; Russia and, 89–92; economic terms of, 93–95; Pacific colonies and Shantung under, 95–98; weakness of, 100; United States defeats, 107–111
Vichy, American diplomatic relations with, 142–144, 174
Virgin Islands, 8, 27
Vladivostok, 90

Washington, Naval Conference, 124; Declaration of, 161–162
Weimar Constitution, 103
Welles, Sumner, 145, 153, 163
Weygand, General, 143, 144, 174
Willkie, Wendell, 136, 201
Wilson, Woodrow, 20, 25, 43; neutrality in First World War, 35–36, 38, 42, 44, 46, 51–52; peace moves, 1916, 48–49; re-elected, 50; objectives in First World War, 53–61; Fourteen Points, 60–62; and Armistice negotiations, 70–78; and Paris Peace Conference, 80, 86–100 *pas-*

*sim;* and postwar American politics, 109–110, 199–200
World Court, 180, 198, 202
World War, First, beginnings, 17; American neutrality in, 31, 34–35, 37–46; progress of, 32–34, 49–51, 66–70; American diplomacy in, 46, 53–62; Armistice, 70–78

YOUNG PLAN, 117
Yugoslavia, 103, 168

ZABERN AFFAIR, 29